LOSING
THE RAT RACE

WINNING
AT LIFE

LOSING THE RAT RACE

WINNING AT LIFE

Marc D. Angel

URIM PUBLICATIONS
Jerusalem • New York

Losing the Rat Race, Winning at Life

by Marc D. Angel

ISBN 965-7108-65-9

Urim Publications, P.O. Box 52287, Jerusalem 91521 Israel

Lambda Publishers Inc.
3709 13th Avenue Brooklyn, New York 11218 U.S.A.
Tel: 718-972-5449, Fax: 718-972-6307, mh@ejudaica.com

www.UrimPublications.com

CONTENTS

Introduction

AN OLD JOKE tells of a pilot who makes an announcement to his passengers: "I have good news and I have bad news. The good news is that we are making excellent time. The bad news is that we don't know where we're going."

The pilot's words might aptly relate to the general human condition in modern times in that we are making excellent time. The technological revolution has vastly increased the speed of human life: we travel faster; we communicate faster; we do almost everything faster.

But we don't always know where we are going.

In our rush to meet the challenges and pressures of life, we may not allow ourselves the time to ponder deeply about the meaning of our lives. Why are we here? What do we hope to accomplish with our lives? Where are we headed? What is genuinely important and what is not genuinely important?

The message of this book is: I have good news, bad news, more bad news and more good news. The good news is that we live in an exciting, fast-paced world that can provide us with many good things. The bad news is that all of us – on some level – find ourselves feeling that we are in a rat race that lacks ultimate meaning. We are so busy trying to succeed that we lose sight of what real success is. The more bad news is that many will stay in the rat race for want of clear direction and willpower.

The more good news is that we all have the ability to get out of the rat race, and live meaningful and happy lives. But we need sharp focus and inner strength.

We can make excellent time and know where we are going.

This book is an attempt to shed light on the obstacles of the rat race; to stimulate thought about the direction of our lives; to help us draw on our strengths so that we might get beyond the rat race.

This is a serious and life-defining agenda. By reading this book and thinking about the topics raised in it, readers are already moving in the right direction.

Chapter One

Losing the Rat Race: Winning at Life

A HIGH SCHOOL COACH took his students out to the running track and led them to the starting line. As the teens stretched into position, the coach called out for them to start. The students took off on their race around the track.

The fastest runners took the lead, straining to keep ahead of the others. As they neared the finish line, one runner pulled ahead and came in first. The others followed as quickly as they could. One runner, though, lagged far behind the others. He finished last by a wide margin.

The coach gathered all the students together. He then declared the slowest student to be the winner, the recipient of the prize. The one who had finished first, in a burst of frustration, called out: "That isn't fair! I won the race. I was the fastest. I finished first. The student you declared winner was the slowest runner, finishing last."

The coach responded: "In this race, the winner was the one who would finish last."

The first-place runner and the rest of the class were unsettled by this answer. They had always been taught that winning a race means coming in first. Now the coach had turned the rules on their head.

The coach said: "We don't ever know who wins unless we first know what the rules are. If the rules of this particular race were different from what you had assumed, that is your problem. Who wins or who loses the race depends on what the rules are."

Who wins or who loses in life depends on what the rules are.

Imagine the following scenario: A robber confronts his victim and takes all the money in his wallet. He then runs away and disappears into a crowd, never to be apprehended for his crime. Who has won this transaction? If winning is determined by who ended up with the most money, then the robber won. If winning means maintaining one's honesty and innocence, then the victim won.

Or, on a grander scale, who were the great "winners" of the last century? If winning is defined as having unlimited power over vast numbers of people, then Lenin, Stalin, Hitler and Pol Pot were among the winners. But if winning is determined by the qualities of righteousness, humanitarianism and purity of soul – then these ruthless tyrants were among the greatest losers in the history of humankind.

What are the rules of life that enable us to determine who has won and who has lost? What are the standards by which we may measure our own levels of success and failure?

For many of us, religious traditions provide the moral framework for life. These traditions make it clear what our goals as human beings should be. We can judge whether or not we are moving in the right direction. For others, a moral framework may be drawn from a philosophy of ethical humanism. But lacking a clear ethical foundation, human life can be destructive and chaotic. Unless human beings agree that the rules of life must include righteousness, kindness and respect for others, the seeds of destruction may be planted within human society. Those who think they are not bound by these rules are people who can be terrorists, murderers, thieves and egotists.

Most civilized human beings have a core set of principles that both enable them to live moral lives and provide them with a yardstick by which to measure the behavior of others. The world religions generally preach a message of righteousness. Humanistic ethical frameworks also argue for suitable behavior, whereby everyone is able to live a good life – not willfully hurting others and not being willfully hurt by others. Yet ethical ideals are one thing; actual human behavior is another. While many people strive to maintain lofty standards, others are ready to compromise or discard ethical values. Society includes the saintly and the wicked, with most people being a combination of the two.

In a free society such as ours, people may espouse a variety of views on moral issues. Confusion and ethical relativism set in. People no longer are sure of what is right and what is wrong; they can find rationalizations to do what they want to do, regardless of whether or not their choices are ethically proper. Society loses its moral compass. It becomes problematic to say who has "won" and who has "lost" at life.

The Talmud (*Pesahim* 50a) relates the story of the seeming death of a son of Rabbi Yehoshua ben Levi. Obviously, the family was mourning the passing of such a promising and learned young man. But then, the son was somehow revived, and the joy was great. Rabbi Yehoshua realized, though, that his son had just had an amazing experience. He had died and thus had experienced life after death. And yet, he was now alive and could describe what he had seen while he was in the next world. "What did you see there?" the Rabbi asked his son. "I saw a topsy-turvy world. Those who are great here are small there; those who are small here are great there." Rabbi Yehoshua told his son: "You have seen the world in its genuine clarity." No, my son, he was saying, you did not see an inverted world; you saw true reality. In this world, humans often misjudge who is actually great or insignificant, powerful or weak. But these misjudgments are rectified in the next world, the true world.

Why do human beings in this world make mistaken judgments about who is winning and who is losing in life? The answer is that we do not always use the correct standards of measurement. We are deluded by external displays of power and glory on the one hand, or by the appearance of powerlessness and failure on the other. But in the "next world," where reality is viewed from God's perspective rather than ours, the truth about who has won and who has lost at life is transparently clear.

In his famous parable of the cave (*The Republic*, Book VII), Plato describes a group of people who have been confined to living in the darkness of a cave, where they have lived since their early childhoods. They have been chained into position, so that they face forward towards a wall of the cave. Behind them is a fire. This source of light reflects off of them, casting their shadows onto the wall in front of them. Since they have never moved and cannot move, their entire sense of reality derives from the images of shadows on the wall. Among themselves, the most honorable and "successful" are those who are quickest to observe the passing shadows, most accurate in their descriptions, and best able to draw conclusions for the future based on their study of the shadows.

But then one person was able to break away from the chains and climb out of the cave. When he was first struck by sunlight, his eyes ached from the glare. In time, thought, he adjusted to the world of sunlight and came to realize that this was true reality; life in the cave had been based on shadows and illusions.

Now, imagine him returning to life in the cave. Since his eyes had grown accustomed to real sunlight, he had difficulty readjusting to the darkness in the cave. He was not as swift to see or describe the images on the wall of the cave. "And if there were a contest, and he had to compete in measuring the shadows with the prisoners who had never moved out of the den… would he not be ridiculous? Men would say of him that up he went and down he came without his eyes; and that it was better not even to think of ascending; and if any one tried to loose another and lead him up to the light, let them only catch the offender, and they would put him to death."

Through this parable, Plato teaches the limitations and folly of those who are only able to judge truth based on the shadows and illusions of our transitory world. These cave dwellers do not realize that they have "lost" in the enterprise of achieving genuine truth. They ostracize those who have seen the sunlight and who have in fact "won." They are ready to execute anyone who dares to challenge their assumptions about truth.

We all have lives to live and we all want to be successful in the art of living. We want to be healthy, happy, prosperous, popular and attractive. We want to have good families, good friends and good reputations. We want our lives to be meaningful to ourselves and to others. When we die, we want to be remembered for the good we have done in our lifetimes. But what are the criteria that make for genuine success? Have we clarified the standards by which we judge success and failure? Are we certain that we see reality, or are we caught up in a web of shadows and illusions?

The noted psychiatrist and author, Dr. Bruno Bettelheim, has observed in his essay, "Education and the Reality Principle": "Yesterday's conviction was that the purpose of all human activity is to gain us eternal salvation; today's popular conviction is that life is a rat race." In the "old days," when religious tradition dominated our civilization, people were concerned that they live righteous lives and avoid sin. They believed that eternal salvation in the next world was ultimately more important than the fleeting trials and travails of this world. But in the modern era, suggests Bettelheim, people have become engrossed in the battles of getting ahead in this world. They either do not believe in the next world or do not care to invest their energies to get there. Since they see their entire existences as being confined to this world, they want to "succeed" here, at whatever price is necessary.

Of course, Bettelheim's pithy observation is stated in a some-what simplistic form. Many moderns do indeed believe in ultimate salvation; many pre-moderns did engage in Machiavellian self-promotion. Nevertheless, the essence of his statement contains a truth that deserves serious consideration. Are we moderns essentially living our lives as though we are in a rat race? Have we lost sight of issues of ultimate meaning in life?

Dr. Viktor Frankl, father of the school of logotherapy in psychia-try, pointed out that moderns are increasingly confronted with "existential vacuum," a sense of meaninglessness and emptiness in life. "In contrast to man in former times, he [the modern] is no longer told by traditions and values what he should do. Now, knowing neither what he must do nor what he should do, he sometimes does not even know what he basically wishes to do. Instead, he wishes to do what other people do – which is con-formism – or he does what other people wish him to do – which is totalitarianism."

While many of us, surely, are not engulfed by existential vacuum, we can hardly avoid being influenced by its manifestations. The ubiquitous pressures of conformity and quasi-totalitarianism (as in cliques, ideological movements and cults) quash individual freedom. It becomes easier to follow along rather than to define and stand up for one's own values. Subtly and not so subtly, this process may alter our views of "winning" and "losing" at life. We may become less centered on ultimate salvation and more en-trenched in the rat race. Our desire to succeed and to excel drives us to want to achieve greatness in those categories that are valued by our peers – even if those categories are ultimately neutral or negative.

If we are not very careful, we let ourselves slide into the rat race. As we compete in the rat race, we may not even realize how thoroughly we have abandoned our inner freedom, our quest for ultimate meaning. We want to win the rat race even if it means compromising or abandoning the values that imbue life with genuine meaning.

Some people wake up one day and ask: Why am I doing this? What is my life all about? How can I get out of this rat race? They respond by trying to reorganize their lives and reclaim their autonomy.

Others may go through life without responding to these questions, ignoring them, suppressing them. They are so busy competing and trying to outdo everyone else that they do not allow themselves the luxury of thinking too deeply about the meaning of life.

The premise of this book is that we cannot genuinely "win" at life unless we "lose" the rat race. Stated another way, a life well lived is characterized by calm wisdom, a transcendental sense of life's meaning, and an ability to love, empathize with and help others. It does not view life as an eternal and meaningless battle to get "ahead."

People in the rat race are busy trying to keep up with and surpass the Joneses. They are driven by jealousy, greed and competitiveness. They do not see ultimate meaning in their lives, but want as much fame, fortune and fun as they can get. People in the rat race usually are not evil or corrupt, although some are. Many are simply drawn into the race because they have not thoroughly thought through their philosophy of life or do not have the independence of spirit to stand up for their values and ideals. They are driven by conformism or quasi-totalitarianism. They surrender their freedom and autonomy in order to play the game of life according to the rules of the rat race.

What are the characteristics of the rat race?

*An inordinate emphasis on external matters – good looks, wealth, power, popularity, fame.

*A profound feeling that life is a great competition, that we must not allow ourselves to fall behind.

*An acceptance of standards set by others; a drive toward conformity even at the risk of betraying one's own values; an internalization of standards that compromise our freedom to make responsible choices.

*A willingness to abandon ethical standards in order to advance oneself.

*A realization at some point and on some level that the rat race is ultimately meaningless. What have I achieved by "winning"? Has "success" brought me real happiness?

Imagine a group of rats in a maze. Each one struggles ferociously to get through the convoluted passageways as fast as possible, to reach the little piece of cheese at the finish line before all the others. The rats use their wits and senses to find the openings in the maze; they follow others whom they trust to be headed in the right direction; they attack those who block their way. They suffer from high anxiety. The one who wins eats the bit of cheese, as the others fight to steal it away. The rats are on the attack and are already struggling to get ahead in the next maze. The "winner" of the first contest hardly has time to digest the bit of cheese before the next race has begun.

Whereas rats are governed by their genes and instincts, human beings are endowed with the freedom to make choices. Certainly, our freedom is not absolute. We, too, are influenced tremendously by our genes and our environments. But we do have the power to make decisions. Free will is an essential component of being an autonomous human being. We have the need to ask "why?" We seek ultimate meaning in life. We can surrender our autonomy by following the will of others or we can assert our freedom by assuming the responsibility of making decisions. We have the ability to succumb to the competition and meaninglessness of the rat race, and we have the ability to achieve freedom and dignity by maintaining our inner cores of freedom and spirituality.

"Losing" the rat race does not mean that we must stop trying to achieve things with our lives. It does not entail a passive quietism, a surrender from the world of competition. On the contrary, the drive for "success" can be a positive element in our lives. Competitiveness can help us and others reach higher levels of achievement than we otherwise could have attained.

"Losing" the rat race means that we do not allow ourselves to be swallowed up by competitiveness, that we maintain our personal autonomy and freedom, that we not become slaves to conformism and totalitarianism. "Winning" at life entails living with a sense of inner purpose and meaning, genuinely loving and being loved, maintaining righteous ethical standards, not being afraid to withstand negative social pressures.

We might know in our minds that it is best for us to lose the rat race and to win at life. Yet so many of us do not integrate this knowledge into our actual patterns of living. We see masses of people running the rat race and we feel drawn to join them. We do not want to be left behind. We do not want to come in last place. We do not want them to think badly of us. In our desire to blend in with and be accepted by others, we gradually internalize the values of the rat race; we abandon or compromise the standards that we know are essential for living a good and righteous life. We leave the light of truth and follow after shadows and illusions.

A rabbinic parable tells of a poor man who was struggling to support his family. He learned of a faraway land that was filled with precious jewels. A ship would soon be leaving for this land and it had room for him as a passenger. But the ship would only return after a long interval; so if the man chose to go to the faraway land, he would have to remain there for a considerable time. His wife agreed that he should make the voyage. He would be able to obtain valuable jewels and bring them back to support his family in wealth and honor.

So the man boarded the ship and was off to make his fortune. Sure enough, the ship arrived at the faraway land, and it was indeed filled with treasures. The earth was covered with diamonds, rubies, emeralds, and all types of precious stones. He hurriedly filled his pockets with jewels; he stuffed his bags with gems. He was now an extraordinarily rich man. He rejoiced in the thought of how wealthy he and his family would be upon his return home.

But in the faraway land, the man soon realized that his precious stones were valueless. They were so abundant and so readily available that no one paid any attention to them. None of the storekeepers would accept them as payment for merchandise. Rather, the currency of this land was wax candles. These were hard to come by and were highly valued by the public. Everyone strove to accumulate as many wax candles as possible; their wealth and power were evaluated by the number of candles they possessed.

It did not take long for the man to recognize his need for wax candles. He worked hard to gain as many as he could. Soon, he had accumulated a large number of them. He emptied his pockets and bags of the diamonds, rubies and emeralds, and filled them instead with wax candles. In this new land, he became wealthy and prominent – very "successful."

Time passed. It was now time for the man to return to his wife and family. The ship was ready to leave. Quickly, the man packed as many wax candles as he could, so that he could bring them back with him. He proudly boarded the ship, laden with as many candles as he could possibly carry.

When he arrived home, his wife eagerly greeted him. She asked to see the treasures he had brought back. Proudly, the man opened his bags and emptied his pockets. He stacked up piles of wax candles.

His wife was astonished. "You spent all that time in the faraway land, a land filled with precious jewels, and you brought back only piles of worthless wax candles? Are you joking with me?"

Then, suddenly, the man realized he had made a terrible mistake. When he had arrived in the faraway land, he knew he was supposed to gather precious gems – but he had soon forgotten his mission. Influenced by the people in that land, he had come to value candles and ignore jewels. He had completely forgotten his original goal. He had thought that by accumulating candles, he had become successful. But now that he had returned home, he realized that he had missed his opportunity to bring back real treasures. Instead, he came back with a pile of nearly worthless candles.

We human beings are placed on earth to attain transcendent treasures – wisdom, love, spiritual insight, moral courage. If we can keep our lives focused on these goals and if we can direct our lives according to these ideals – then we "win" at life. But if we come to ascribe greater value to mundane attainments – wealth, power, fame – then we may find ourselves having accumulated things that are ultimately of little worth.

Winning at life means keeping focused on what is truly important and not getting sidetracked by external glitz. Winning is not a one time event, but an ongoing way of life.

Chapter Two

The Rules of the Rat Race

THE BIBLE RECOUNTS the story of how Abraham purchased the cave of Machpelah as a burial place for his wife Sarah. The land had been the property of Efron the Hittite. When Abraham first mentions to Efron his interest in buying the cave, Efron courteously offers to give Abraham the land as a gift. Abraham, with matching courtesy, declines Efron's offer, stating that he wants to pay for the cave. Hearing this, Efron says: "My lord, hearken unto me. A piece of land worth four hundred shekels of silver, what is that between me and you? Bury therefore your dead."

At this point in the narrative, Abraham might have been expected to reject such a high price; he might have put forward a counter offer, in the style of Middle Eastern bargaining. He knew that Efron's original offer to give him the land for free was only a ceremonial ruse. He also knew that it was customary for sellers to start with high prices and then reduce the sum after a process of negotiation. But what did Abraham do? "And Abraham hearkened unto Efron; and Abraham weighed to Efron the silver, which he had named in the hearing of the children of Heth, four hundred shekels of silver, current money with the merchant" (Genesis 23:16). Not only did Abraham pay the full price that Efron had set; he paid in the best available currency.

Efron must have gone home very happy that day. He had made a handsome profit. Moreover, he must have congratulated himself on how clever he was to outwit Abraham. Efron had won an impressive business victory.

Looking carefully at the Hebrew text, classic rabbinic interpreters noticed that throughout the narrative, Efron's name was spelled in its full form (five letters). But when the Bible states that Abraham "weighed to Efron the silver" – in that one instance Efron's name was spelled in a shorter form (four letters). The rabbinic lesson drawn from this was that it was Efron, in fact, who "lost" in this transaction in that he was diminished by it. While he had begun his discussion with Abraham by offering to give the field to him at no cost, at its conclusion Efron had exacted a very high sum. On the surface, he appeared to be generous and courteous. But when it came to the actual negotiations, Efron began with an exaggerated price, demonstrating that he had no genuine interest in acting kindly to Abraham. For Efron, business is business; compassion and kindness play no role. On the other hand, Abraham showed himself to be courteous and generous throughout the transaction. He did not wish to lower himself by bargaining down the high price that Efron had requested. He paid in full and in the best currency; he asked for and received no favors from Efron.

Efron's name was spelled with a letter missing as a reminder to readers that Efron had something missing in his approach to life. He was playing by the rules of the rat race: win the game, come out ahead, outsmart others. By these rules, he indeed defeated Abraham. But Abraham, a dignified and princely man, conducted himself by the rules of honor and self respect. He knew that "winning" at life entailed rising above the rat race. Abraham paid Efron all that he asked, but Efron was revealed as a greedy hypocrite and had a letter dropped from his name. He was a lesser person, even though he himself might not have realized it.

Efron, by this interpretation, is an example of someone who takes the short view of "success." The goal is to win a transaction, even if in the process one loses his sense of honor and self respect. Don't confuse such people with those who ascribe to the long view of things, those who honor the importance of integrity, dignity and a good name. Those who take the short view want to win by the rules of the rat race. They don't want to think of a different and higher set of rules.

I know of a landlady who found a legal loophole that enabled her to evict tenants who had been living in her building for nearly twenty-eight years. The tenants had always paid rent on time and had given her no trouble over all those years. But she could get a much higher rent from new tenants. Instead of speaking to her long-term tenants and negotiating a suitable rent hike, she simply had her lawyer send an eviction notice. For the landlady, the issue had nothing to do with respect, sympathetic human understanding, loyalty or decency. The issue was one-dimensional: money. She could get more rent from a new tenant. It was not even a matter of the landlady needing to have more money to support herself. She was well-off financially. She was in her sixties, unmarried, with no children or natural heirs. She told an acquaintance that she planned to leave her fortune to her cat!

So the long-standing tenants were unceremoniously turned out of their apartment. By the rules of the rat race, the landlady won. By the rules of civility and simple humanity, though, she lost very badly. Like Efron, she was diminished by the transaction. Whatever she gained in money, she lost far more in honor, reputation and self-respect.

Greed can result not only in unsavory behavior, but also in illegal and dangerous activity. Blinded by the desire to gain money, a person might make decisions that are dishonest and harmful to others. A blatant example of this tendency occurred during the American mobilization for war in the early 1940s. It was found that a number of manufacturers were supplying faulty military equipment to the United States government. A senate commission, under the chairmanship of then-Senator Harry S. Truman, conducted investigations.

The manufacturer of the B-26 bomber admitted that the wings of the aircraft had not been built wide enough, and posed a serious safety threat to the pilots of those planes. When Truman asked why the wings had not been corrected, the manufacturer answered that the plans were already too advanced to make changes; and besides, his company already had the government contract! An inspector of airplane engines of another company noted that inspectors had let faulty engines pass inspection; he admitted that he had also done so, even though he had two nephews in the

Army Air Corps. The goal, plain and simple, was to increase profits. This goal eclipsed both moral and ethical concerns.

The Truman commission looked into the circumstances of a newly constructed tanker that broke in two. The steel plate manufactured for the ship's construction had not been made according to government standards. The manufacturers substituted cheaper steel, but claimed to have delivered the higher-grade steel that the government had ordered and paid for. A spokesman for the company admitted a "misrepresentation" but denied that the inferior steel posed a problem in the shipbuilding process. Throughout the hearings, it became obvious that leading business people were attempting to deceive the government in order to maximize their companies' profits. That their decisions led to the building of inferior equipment that would jeopardize the lives of American military personnel did not seem to be an overriding concern to them.

Were they cruel people who plotted the deaths of young American pilots, soldiers and sailors? No. They were morally weak people who were blinded by their greed for quick profits. They did not give adequate thought to what the consequences of their decisions would mean for the lives of others or the welfare of the nation.

By the rules of the rat race, a person's focus should be on gathering as much money and property as possible. As in the children's game, the one who ends up with the most marbles is the winner. But, as has been pointed out by a wise observer, the one who has gathered the most marbles still dies – and is not able to take the marbles with him. Gathering marbles is not a worthy end in itself;

likewise, material possessions must be viewed as a means to an end. Money is not wealth – it is potential wealth. It affords a person the opportunity to have the things and do the things that are genuinely important in life.

Winning at life does not mean having the most material possessions. It comes, rather, from being a genuinely sharing and generous person, one who loves and is loved.

People in the rat race, eager to amass as much money as possible, do not give charity proportional to their wealth – or sometimes do not give charity at all. One wealthy politician, whose annual income was reported to be more than twenty million dollars, listed charitable tax deductions in the amount of two thousand dollars! A mayor of a large city, whose annual salary was above $125,000, listed his annual charitable contributions at several hundred dollars and some old clothes that he donated to the Salvation Army. These highly successful politicians show how truly selfish they are by their stingy charitable contributions. They think that they win more by keeping more; but, in fact, their inability to give generously demonstrates a serious flaw in their personalities.

An important characteristic of righteous people is generosity. Good people want to share with others, to help the less fortunate, to do what they can to make a better society. Rat race people are so self-centered, they find it difficult to spend their own money in order to help others. They do give charity, though, when it serves their purposes – i.e., to gain tax breaks, to build up their reputations, to give themselves more power and influence.

Sometimes, people in the rat race receive a rude awakening. They see that they have been worshipping false gods; they try to salvage their lives and their reputations. It has been reported that Alfred Nobel, founder of the Nobel prizes, had such an experience. One morning, he read his own obituary in the newspaper! Someone had erroneously informed the paper that Nobel had died. The obituary was not flattering. It noted that Nobel had accumulated great wealth through the manufacture of dynamite; that working conditions in the dynamite factories were less than satisfactory; that a number of workers had been killed at their jobs due to the lack of safety provisions. In short, Nobel had made a lot of money at the expense of others – even at the cost of some of their lives. Putting down the obituary, Nobel started to think: "Is this the way I want to be remembered by posterity? As a rich industrialist who did not show proper concern for his workers? As a person who looked out only for himself?"

Presumably, he realized the need to be more concerned for others; there were more important things in life than accumulating wealth. He decided to establish the Nobel prizes as a way of fostering peace and learning, as a contribution to help the world. Surely, he gained reputation and stature from his gifts. Yet the most important gain for him was an internal awareness that he had been running the wrong race. He achieved more from giving than from taking.

While some people have generous dispositions and clearly understand that giving is more virtuous than taking, others have a lot of trouble with this concept. They say: What's mine is mine, what's yours is yours – and don't talk to me about sharing.

Yet sharing and compassion are at the heart of living a good, happy life. One wins at life in proportion to the ability to love and care for others.

The Kabbalah teaches us that two tendencies operate in the world: the power of receiving and the power of giving. The power of receiving is characteristic of all worldly creatures; all receive sustenance from the Almighty. Human beings also receive assistance and support from other human beings. We could not live without receiving – from our parents, spouses, teachers, friends, clients, customers, business and professional associates. We survive and thrive because we take so much from so many.

The power of giving represents the other side of the pendulum. We do not only take from others; we are also obliged to give. We provide sustenance, guidance and assistance to others, helping them to live better lives.

The power of receiving connects humans with the animal and mineral worlds. Although necessary for our existence, it is not an expression of humanity at its loftiest. The power of giving is modeled after the ultimate Giver, God, Who gives without needing to receive anything back in return. The more we utilize the power of giving, the more we emulate God.

If someone takes but does not give back commensurately, the Kabbalah describes him as one who has eaten the "bread of shame." He has not earned his bread; he has taken beyond that to which he was entitled. He was dominated by the power of receiving rather than the power of giving. He thinks that he has come out ahead because he has received more than he has given. But, in fact, he has sacrificed his human dignity to his greed. He is guilty of eating the bread of shame; he has proven himself to be an unworthy person.

Most people have a fairly objective way of measuring their own generosity. Each year, we prepare our financial data for income taxes. We can see very clearly how much we have spent, on what we have spent, and how much we have given for charitable purposes. Indeed, the way we spend our money is a fairly accurate indication of our moral values; it is a clearer indication of who we are than what we may think and say about ourselves.

To win at life means to avoid eating the bread of shame. For people in the rat race, though, the object of life is exactly the opposite: to eat the bread of shame – to take in far more than what we have given, to come out ahead materially in every transaction.

One feature of the rat race is that participants strive to gather as much as they can for themselves and to keep up with or get ahead of their competitors. Whether it be in business or academia, the arts or sciences, sports or entertainment, rat race people feel driven to outdo others, to come out ahead. They want more awards, bigger houses, fancier cars, more luxuries, greater reputations. They seldom stop to ask whether the rat race has ultimate meaning, whether it is all worth the sacrifice. A wit once remarked that he had never met anyone who, upon reviewing life in old age, said: "I wish I had spent more time in the office!" No, they wish they had spent more time with their families and friends; more time doing something good for society; more time in study and reflection. Now that they near the conclusions of their lives, they realize that they had been busy collecting counterfeit wealth when they should have been gathering genuine treasures.

What, then, drives people to be part of the rat race? Why doesn't everyone simply step away from the self-destructive strife? Why are they motivated by the notion that life is a great competition, that they must not fall behind? And why don't they foster the spirit of generosity within themselves? Why doesn't everyone strive mightily to avoid eating the bread of shame?

These are complex questions. They touch on a deep enigma of the human predicament: If people know what is right, why do they actually do what is wrong?

One reason may be that human beings are innately competitive. Just like the other creatures of the animal world, humans battle for sustenance, mating partners and dominance. If the natural world operates by the principle of "survival of the fittest," shouldn't we expect the same rule to apply to humans?

Indeed, when human beings follow their animal natures, they are prone to violence and cruelty. Human history is replete with wars, persecutions, torture of enemies, family strife, criminal activity and fierce competition in almost all fields of endeavor. The wild popularity of sex, sports and violence in the media are perhaps the most obvious public manifestations of the widespread drive to compete, to conquer, to vanquish. These themes would not be so pervasive and popular unless they addressed the basic emotions of their vast audiences.

It is natural, then, for us to compete and strive to win. Competition in and of itself is not necessarily destructive. In fact, it can improve us individually and as a society. The desire to achieve great things can push us to the limits of our abilities. Competition, when properly directed, is a valuable spur to personal development. Serious problems arise, though, when competitiveness becomes so obsessive that it is destructive to oneself and to others. Our challenge as responsible human beings is not to negate the reality of competition, but rather to learn how to channel our competitive drives in positive, constructive ways.

My golf coach in high school taught us that to play our best game of golf, we should concentrate on trying to achieve or beat par. We should not pay attention to whether the other players are doing better or worse than we are. This lesson applies to all of life. Our goal should certainly be to do our very best in whatever we undertake. But our focus should be on our own game, not on the games of others. We must learn to measure our successes not by comparing ourselves to others, but by comparing our accomplishments with what our own abilities and talents should have accomplished. Have we achieved our own potential? If we keep this in mind, we can win at life and avoid being swallowed up by the rat race.

I used to be a member of the New York Road Runners Club. My greatest running accomplishment was to complete the New York City Marathon in 1983. I used to participate regularly in shorter runs – four miles, six miles, ten miles. I enjoyed the challenge of keeping in training and drawing on my physical strength and will power to reach the finish line. At some point, the Road Runners Club made an innovation: they sent all runners a printout of their individual times and their ranking among others of the same age range. They thought that this information would stimulate competitiveness; runners would try to run faster so as to get higher up on the list of finishers. But, at least in my case, this innovation had the opposite result. I had never cared to know my ranking among other runners; I wasn't competing against them – I was competing only against myself. My satisfaction had nothing to do with what place I finished. If I ran well, if I felt I was improving – then I was happy, even if I would have finished last.

Although the competitive drive is best when self-directed, it would be unrealistic to think that human beings will live their lives entirely free of competition with others. Even so, competitiveness does not have to rule us. We are, after all, different from the other members of the animal kingdom. We have the power to think conceptually, to plan, to build, to create technology, to foster spiritual life, to engage in the arts and sciences. We remember and learn from our past. We envision our future. We record our teachings and insights for posterity. While our competitive drive makes us receptive to the rat race, it does not condemn us to it. We do have the power to make choices, to exercise free will. This is the source of human freedom and distinctiveness.

So why do so many of us continue to participate in the rat race, to the detriment of our mental, spiritual and emotional health?

This brings us to a fascinating observation. On the one hand, participants in the rat race want to win, to surpass others. They want to stand out. Yet, on the other hand, such people display an opposite tendency: they want to conform, they want to do what everyone else is doing, they don't want to be left behind or ridiculed for going in a different direction. While the drive to beat the competition is an incentive to join the rat race, the drive to conform is what locks people in it.

The psychologist, Solomon Asch, conducted experiments in the early 1950s in which he demonstrated the power of social pressure on people's opinions. He recruited volunteers for a "visual perception study." Each volunteer arrived at the experiment room and found seven other subjects (all part of Asch's experiment team) seated in a row. The experimenter showed the participants a pair of cards, asking them to determine which of three comparison lines on one card was the same length as a standard line on the other card. The first seven people gave the correct answer, as did the last one. This process was repeated several times. But then the experimenter, using another card, asked participants to determine the correct matching line. The first seven participants, who were part of the experiment, all gave the incorrect answer. The subject of the experiment now had to answer. On the one hand, it was fairly obvious that the first seven had answered incorrectly. On the other hand, the subject felt some self-doubt since all the others had given the same (incorrect) answer.

Each subject participated in this experiment several times. Approximately 75% of them went along with the group's consensus at least once, even though they were giving the answer they thought was expected rather than the answer they themselves had determined to be true. Considering all trials combined, subjects followed the incorrect answers of the group about one-third of the time.

Subsequent studies by other researchers have demonstrated that the tendency towards conformity within a group – even when one feels the group is wrong – is intensified when one feels part of the group and feels a commitment to it. Additionally, people are more likely to conform to group norms when the group members are friends or those with whom they have (or want) a sense of cohesiveness.

Even in a society such as the United States, where individuality is encouraged, the pressures towards conformity are quite powerful. People will go against their own knowledge and values in order to fit in with the larger group. They will smoke, drink alcoholic beverages in excess, engage in promiscuous sexual encounters, cheat in business – all in order to blend in with their chosen peer group.

The conformity syndrome is vastly exacerbated when the control group is not just one's peers, but mass culture as well. Thus, in American society we are constantly bombarded by the media – and by the values and styles they promote. Success is equated with wealth, sex and power. The media present the "ideal" images of beauty, luxury and social success. These images are pervasive, and it is all but impossible to escape their influence. Children grow up thinking that they can "win" in their lives if they conform to the popularly promoted standards of success. These standards are almost invariably materialistic and hedonistic. If you have a lot of money, live in a big house, wear designer clothes, have a lot of sexual encounters, travel with the jet set – then you are "winning" the rat race. But if you live humbly, concentrate on developing your spiritual and intellectual life, believe in traditional moral standards, grow old without hiding your gray hair – then you are not part of the mainstream. You are falling behind, you are not cool, you are "losing" the rat race, you are a failure.

The forces that draw us towards conformity are so great that many people are willing to go against their own values, reason and common sense in order to adopt the popular norms. Sometimes they feel guilty at their self betrayal. Sometimes they convince themselves that they are not betraying themselves at all, but that they have adopted a better system of values and truth.

The absurdity of conforming to the values of the rat race is illustrated by the stereotypical nouveaux riches, people who were poor but who have now come into huge sums of money. What is their goal? They want to show others that they have achieved success. And how do they do this? They buy the biggest, gaudiest and most expensive things they can find. They think that they will thereby impress others, showing them just how rich they have become.

This tendency is apparent not only in those who have become rich. It also operates among those who are not particularly affluent but who feel they must impress others by flaunting material wealth – i.e., poor or moderate income people who carry huge boom boxes, insist on wearing only designer clothes, sport expensive jewelry and drive expensive cars.

The common denominator of these examples is that the people involved have come to determine "success" on the basis of external material things. They have been swept up in the pervasive messages of the media, entertainment, fashion and advertising companies. They have accepted the rules of the rat race. In the process, they have surrendered some of their autonomy, freedom and integrity. The deeper they get into the rat race, the more they lose. While they are busy trying to luxuriate their bodies, they forget to provide adequate nourishment for their souls.

Alan Watts, a thoughtful exponent of human spirituality, has wisely observed: "For when man no longer confuses himself with the definition of himself that others have given him, he is at once universal and unique." People in the rat race let others define who they are. They constantly strive to conform to those ideas, standards and behaviors that will (in their minds) ingratiate them with or make them more similar to the dominant group. They come to define their happiness and success by popular materialistic and hedonistic standards. In so doing, they not only betray themselves, but they sacrifice much of their genuine universality and uniqueness.

Thus far, we have discussed the allure of the rat race in terms of the human competitive drive as well as the drive towards conformity. But we must also discuss another vital aspect of the human character: the drive to be part of a crowd.

Elias Canetti, in his landmark book *Crowds and Power*, explores the psychological/sociological factors relating to the phenomenon of crowds among human beings. In short, the individual person somehow feels stronger and greater when he is part of a large group of people. A crowd always wants to grow; it welcomes new members; it seems to gain a life of its own. Within the crowd, all participants feel a sense of equality. "It is for the sake of this equality that people become a crowd and they tend to overlook anything which might detract from it." In the crowd, there are no distinctions between rich and poor, wise and ordinary: all share a feeling of equality by the mere virtue of their bodies being counted into the numbers of the crowd. Individuality is not important; rather it is adding one's presence to the blurry mass of the crowd that is essential.

The crowd loves density. The crowd needs a direction, it moves towards a goal. The direction, shared by all of its members, strengthens the feeling of equality and solidarity.

Canetti describes a variety of types of crowds, but all share the above-mentioned features. People want to transcend the limits of their own individuality by blending into a larger mass of human beings. By being part of a crowd, one tends to fade away as a distinctive individual, merging instead into a larger, more powerful entity. A member of the crowd feels validated and protected by the group.

Let us consider for a moment an example of what Canetti calls a closed crowd. A crowd gathers at a stadium to watch a sporting event. The fans gain enthusiasm as they root for their teams. All fans feel part of their teams; they participate vicariously in the action on the field. For the duration of the game, they are all equal, they cheer in unison, they rise to their feet at moments of excitement. In a certain sense, they lose themselves in the excitement of the event. When the game is over, they shout: "We won!" or they glumly confess: "We lost." Of course, they have no real right to say "we" won or "we" lost, because they in fact have not been playing the game themselves. The athletes alone may truly say that they won or lost, because they were doing the actual playing. The fans are only bystanders. Yet the fans – members of a closed crowd – have so fully identified with the players that they say with perfect honesty that "we" won or "we" lost. The crowd has transformed them from discreet individuals to a mass of fans who identify with the players on the field.

Many people find enormous satisfaction in being part of a crowd. It expands their lives, it gives them a feeling of importance and equality, it gives them a goal and direction. And in all of this, they do not have to take personal responsibility. They merely have to allow themselves to be swept up by the energy of the crowd. While part of the crowd, they care little about their uniqueness and universality; they care only about blending into the crowd.

Since human beings are so predisposed to being part of a crowd, the rat race has a powerful appeal. The rat race, like the crowd, wants to grow, loves density, needs a direction. In the rat race, though, the sense of equality is not clear. On the one hand, participants want to outdo others; they struggle for superiority, not equality. On the other hand, since the rat race is dominated by the forces of conformity, participants feel a sense of equality when they share the same values, styles and behaviors as other participants.

It is clear, then, that various powerful factors – competitiveness, conformity and crowds – draw us into the orbit of the rat race. It takes considerable inner strength to withstand the pressures. It often seems easier or more expedient simply to surrender our autonomy and let ourselves give in to the desire to compete, to conform, to lose ourselves in a crowd.

We need to remind ourselves that loss of personal autonomy from time to time does not necessarily lead to the undermining of individuality. But if surrendering autonomy becomes the pattern of one's life, then one is on a dangerous, self-destructive course.

Chapter Three

The Rat Race for Popularity and Social Acceptance

W<small>HEN</small> I <small>WAS A CHILD</small>, I attended the Seattle Hebrew Day School. It was a small and relatively homogeneous school; in my class, we had a total of six students.

After graduation from the Day School at the end of eighth grade, I went on to attend public school for grades nine through twelve – Sharples Junior High School for grade nine and Franklin High School for grades ten through twelve. When I began studies at Sharples Junior High School, I found myself in an altogether different setting from grade school. I now attended a school that had several thousand students of various races, religions and backgrounds. This was a dramatic introduction to "the real world."

As is true of most teenagers, I wanted to be accepted in my new society. I was anxious to gain friends and become part of the school community. One of the first moral dilemmas I faced in public school related to a fellow student who had, for whatever reasons, been deemed by the other students as an outcast. This student was isolated and rejected by the other students, and they used to say that he was "contaminated." Anyone who even touched him was also considered to have become "contaminated." I well remember him running through the halls trying to touch people, and how everyone would scream and run away at his approach. I was never able to learn from anyone why this outcast was "contaminated," what he had done wrong, why he was rejected. He did have a somewhat odd appearance, but so did many other students, none of whom was singled out as being "contaminated."

One morning, I was standing in the hall with a group of friends. I was still a newcomer to the school and was eager to be accepted by others. As we stood talking, the outcast student suddenly turned up next to our group. Before I knew it, he stretched his arm out to me and asked me to shake his hand.

I experienced a very long moment. I had to make a painful decision. On the one hand, if I shook his hand, I would be ostracized by the very group of students I was trying to befriend. The "normal" pattern in the school was for students to avoid touching the outcast, and also to insult him or flee from him. To shake his hand would mean that I was allowing myself to become "contaminated." On the other hand, the outcast student's eyes implored me to recognize him as a fellow human being who was entitled to recognition and acceptance. I had nothing personally against this fellow. My family and religious tradition taught compassion for the stranger, the downtrodden and the oppressed.

I had only an instant to reconcile this conflict and respond. And I did shake his hand. My fellow students laughed at me and mocked me; they moved down the hall away from me and told others of my being "contaminated." The outcast student looked thankfully into my eyes and then ran away to chase after other students.

If the story stopped there, I think that most would agree that I had demonstrated a high level of moral courage. I did the right thing even though I knew I was risking my own social acceptance. I had defied the rules of the rat race by forfeiting an opportunity to gain popularity with my peers.

But the story did not end there.

Before going to my next class, I hurried to the washroom and scrubbed my hands with soap and water. In some horrible way, I had internalized the popular mythology that this student was actually contaminated. I had risen above, but not totally escaped, the pernicious prejudices of my classmates.

All of us have faced similar dilemmas, conflicts in our moral development. We have found ourselves having to decide: Should we do the morally correct thing or should we succumb to expedience? Should we take a possibly unpopular stand or should we simply try to blend in with the crowd, to look the other way?

Robert Coles, in his book, *The Moral Life of Children*, described moral dilemmas faced by a number of children who lived in particularly difficult circumstances. He spent time, for example, with a young black girl in the South who was the first black student to attend a public school that had been ordered to become integrated. Each day, this girl faced horrific verbal assaults by the students and adults of the public school community. She needed police protection simply to attend school. Coles asked her why she went through all this suffering – why didn't she decide to drop out of that school and attend an all-black school where she would be comfortable? The girl answered quite simply: Her mother had taught her that God wanted everyone to do the right thing. If we do the right thing, God will help us. She drew tremendous moral strength from this lesson. She gained the inner resolve to suffer terrible abuse and injustice because she believed she was doing the right thing. She was willing to pay whatever price was necessary in order to combat the scourge of racial discrimination.

Coles also described the situation of a white boy who befriended a black student in a newly integrated school. He did so at the risk of alienating all of his white friends. His own father strongly opposed his associating with the black student. Yet this white student somehow knew what was right, and he was willing to assume the consequences of doing the right thing.

Each human being is engaged in an ongoing struggle to develop and maintain moral character. We each recognize the importance of being an individual even in a crowd of people; the need to be sensitive to the feelings of others; the ability to allow others to be different from ourselves; the ability to learn from mistakes, to think beyond ourselves so that we may exert a positive influence on society at large.

I assume that everyone reading this book has a strong sense of what is morally right and what is morally wrong. Intellectually, almost all of us will generally come up with the correct answers to moral dilemmas. However, when we actually find ourselves in the midst of moral conflict, it is not always our sense of right and wrong that prevails. Often enough we are swayed by other, usually social, considerations.

Alexander Solzhenitsyn has pointed out that life might be much easier if we were able to differentiate clearly between good and evil people. All we would have to do is separate the evil ones from the rest of us. "But the line dividing good and evil acts through the heart of every human being. And who is willing to destroy a piece of his own heart?" With each person imbued with the forces of good and evil, the dividing line between the two is often blurred. Choosing the morally proper path is not always an easy matter, since we have the competing interests of "evil" tugging away at us.

Some years ago, a Wall Street tycoon was indicted for engaging in large-scale insider trading transactions. He was asked to explain why he had transmitted insider information to others when he knew this was illegal and immoral. His answer was candid: "There had been many years of friendship. We were friends."

When faced with a conflict between the morally right thing to do and maintaining friendships, this person chose to maintain his friendships. Is he an evil person? I don't think so. But like so many people caught in similar dilemmas, he succumbed to moral weakness in order to become or remain popular. Thus moral judgment can be impaired by the drive to get along, to maintain social status, for it is common for humans to want to win approval from their peers.

The urge to conform to the expectations of peers is a powerful factor in keeping one in the rat race. It takes a clear sense of right and wrong, coupled with moral courage, to resist being swept up by the crowd. When we are not sure of our own footing, we run the risk of slipping.

Although everyone faces the conflict of being in the rat race or maintaining freedom and autonomy, some cultural situations exacerbate the decision-making process. We are, after all, greatly influenced by our families and social contexts.

The anthropologist Margaret Mead described various types of cultural patterns in her book, *Culture and Commitment: A Study of the Generation Gap*. One of them, the cofigurative culture, is characterized by a loss of authority by the elders. The young generation keenly feels the winds of change. They see the elders as being old-fashioned, relics of a failed past. The young want to break away and join the adventure of living in modernity. They want to have choices and make decisions on their own. Instead of venerating the elders as the ultimate source of wisdom and authority, they see the elders as an embarrassing burden.

A vivid example of a cofigurative culture is the generation of immigrants. The immigrants have come to a new land where their language, culture and traditions are not dominant and not highly valued. They are deeply rooted in the traditional qualities of their home countries; at the same time, they understand the need for their children to adapt to the new culture. In this situation, the elders lose authority; they themselves are conflicted about the best way to bridge past and future.

Some elders may insist that their children follow the old ways without any deviation. But the children see their new friends and neighbors who live in a different style from that which their elders are impressing upon them. The elders are not reinforced by society, and in fact are at odds with society.

Some elders, facing the new situation, may consciously or subconsciously realize that their way of life has come to an end. For their children to be successful in the new world, they will have to abandon the old ways. These elders encourage their children to adopt the mores of the new land, freeing them as much as possible from the old-world baggage that might hold back their progress. The elders make the fateful decision to be the last generation in the tradition of their people; they are martyrs to what they think is the progress of their children.

Other elders try to strike a balance between maintaining and transmitting the old traditions, while at the same time making accommodations to the new situation. They may realize that their traditional language, dress and music will die out among the younger generations, but they still strive to pass on beliefs, customs and practices.

In a cofigurative culture, though, the decisions about what to maintain and what to leave behind are made by the younger generation, not the elders. This becomes a major source of intergenerational conflict.

A cofigurative culture must deal with feelings of betrayal, guilt and shame. The younger generation rejects important aspects of the culture of the elders and the elder generation is powerless to halt the process. The new arbiters of mores for the young generation are their native-born peers and the popular mass culture that engulfs them all.

The pathos of the generation of elders and the confusion of the new generation are poignantly reflected in a scene in Amy Tan's novel, *The Joy Luck Club*. The story deals with a group of Chinese families who emigrated to San Francisco. While the elders maintained strong memories of their home world in China, their children attended American schools and were well into the process of Americanization. The main character, Jing-mei, is known by her American name, June.

Several months after the death of her mother, June meets with her mother's group of friends. In the course of their conversation, she is struck by the realization that the elders are troubled by her Americanization: "They are frightened. In me, they see their own daughters, just as ignorant, just as unmindful of all the truths and hopes they have brought to America. They see daughters who grow impatient when their mothers talk in Chinese, who think they are stupid when they explain things in fractured English…. They see daughters who will bear grandchildren born without any connecting hope passed from generation to generation."

A cofigurative culture is confronted in a serious way with discontinuity. The central question is: Will our culture survive? Have we reached the end of our group's historical cohesiveness? What does the future hold for our coming generations? Do we even dare to hope for future generations beyond our children? The answers to these questions will come as a result of the individual decisions of group members.

Sometimes individuals make their decisions not on the basis of well-reasoned arguments, but from a desire to assimilate into the dominant culture. Their drive to be accepted is so powerful that it leads to a betrayal of their own culture and background.

Mohandas Gandhi told of a well-known Hindu in India who chose to be converted to Christianity as a way of raising his social status. After he was baptized, the new Christian ate beef and drank liquor, and began to wear European clothing, including a hat. In order to further prove his allegiance to his adopted religion, he attempted to create distance between himself and his past. It was not long before he had "begun abusing the religion of his ancestors, their customs and their country." His betrayal of his native heritage must certainly have brought scorn upon him from the Hindus, and it is also likely that the European Christians did not fully accept him either. Such individuals live in a sort of cultural limbo, impelled by the overwhelming urge to be accepted by their chosen group. Their situation would seem comical if it were not so tragic.

The Fox Indians of the Great Lakes region told an ironic anecdote describing their cultural dilemma. An Indian became a practicing Christian, went to church, gave up smoking and drinking, and acted kindly to everyone. When he died, he went to the Indian hereafter but was turned away because he was a Christian. He then went to the Christian heaven but was rejected because he was an Indian. He then went to hell, but was not admitted because he was a good man. So he came alive again and went to the Buffalo Dance and other dances, and he taught his children to do likewise.

In other words, when one betrays his/her own traditions in order to assimilate into a dominant culture, happiness is not necessarily the result. Before one makes life-changing decisions, one should be very sure that adequate thought and analysis have been applied. Is one doing this because it is genuinely the right thing or is he simply participating in the rat race – trying to conform, to keep up, to be accepted?

We are all familiar with the story of Faust, a man who so wanted to be famous and successful that he made a pact with the devil. He sold his soul in order to attain glory in his lifetime on earth. He defined success as gaining the admiration of the public and he wanted to attain this at whatever price he had to pay.

Faust indeed gained fame, although not enough to make him feel genuinely happy and fulfilled. (When one is greedy, one never seems able to satisfy one's cravings. One always wants more.) When he nears the end of his life and has to give his soul over to the devil, Faust is revealed as a tragic, hopelessly misguided figure. He had given up so much in order to attain so little.

Faust is a classic illustration of one who devoted himself to winning the rat race and thereby lost at life. He was willing to sacrifice his soul to achieve a seductive, but destructive, goal. His choice gave him little happiness in this world and eternal torment in the next world.

When we are pulled by the forces of the rat race to compromise ourselves for the sake of fame, popularity or social acceptance, we should remember Faust. Then we should think carefully about our own souls.

Chapter Four

More About the Rat Race: People as Things

WE HAVE SEEN that the rules of the rat race call for an inordinate emphasis on external shows of "success." Participants are imbued with the feeling that life is a great competition. They want to keep up and to win on whatever level is possible, and they accept the standards of "winning" that are set by peers or popular mass culture. The drive to compete or to conform can overwhelm their senses of morality and decency.

Another feature of the rat race is the process of dehumanization of others – and ultimately, of oneself. In order to get ahead in the rat race, one sometimes has to hurt others, push them aside, step on them or exploit them for one's own advantage. To do this without feeling guilty, one needs to avoid thinking too carefully or sympathetically about his or her competitors. The competitors are not seen as fellow human beings who have feelings and needs, but rather as tools to be used or obstacles to be overcome.

In his famous book *I and Thou*, the philosopher Martin Buber pointed out that at their best, human relationships involve mutual knowledge and respect, treating oneself and others as valuable persons. Certainly, there are times when human relationships do not exist on this lofty level, when we see the other person not as a Thou but as an It. The others become objects. They exist to fulfill a need for us. We are not interested in their humanity, but only in their functional ability to serve us. Much of human interrelationship exists on this level. We need others to cook, to clean, to repair, to be our customers, to provide us with things we need and want. In all of these functional relationships, we are less concerned about the Thou of the others than their ability to serve our interests.

A problem arises, though, if we come to relate to others almost exclusively as objects. This is a signal of a breakdown in society, a breakdown within each person. As Buber has written: "When a culture is no longer centered in a living and continually renewed relational process, it freezes into the It-world, which is broken only intermittently by the eruptive, glowing deeds of solitary spirits." As we dehumanize others, we also engage in the process of dehumanizing ourselves. We make our peace with living in an It-world, using others as things and in turn being used by them for their purposes. This is the basic pattern that prevails in the rat race.

A certain photographer practices his art by taking pictures of large groups of naked people. He recently planned to photograph such a group in Times Square, New York City. The city blocked his plan, objecting that the proposed shot would cause massive traffic disruptions in an already congested part of town. The photographer challenged the city in court, arguing his First Amendment right of freedom of expression. He portrayed himself as a martyr on behalf of civil liberties – what right had the city to suppress his artistic expression? While this dispute was going on, *The New York Times* printed an article in which it quoted the photographer's explanation of his artistic methods. He said that his photography sought to teach people to see naked humans as objects of art, not objects of sex. This was his justification for his modernistic artistic style.

What the photographer said he was doing was treating human beings as objects of art. But should human beings be so treated? Isn't it just as degrading to think of humans as objects of art as objects of sex? Shouldn't human beings be thought of as subjects, as dignified beings endowed with meaning?

Characteristic of the rat race, much of modern society tends to view people as objects. One aspect of this tendency is seeing people primarily as agents of production. When they are more productive, they are more "successful"; when they are not productive, they lose their status. Moreover, in the quest for "success," people seem to be in a rush; they do not have the time or interest for serious interpersonal relationships. Respect and loyalty towards others decline; self-aggrandizement and self-interest grow. Relationships increasingly fall into the category of I-It, not I-Thou.

Erich Fromm has noted that, "We have become things and our neighbors have become things. The result is that we feel powerless and despise ourselves for our impotence." Fromm's point is that treating ourselves and others as objects, as Its, is inherently degrading and destructive.

I think that all of us will agree that each human being wants to be loved and respected as a Thou, and wants to have relationships with others on an I-Thou level. But such relationships demand commitments of emotion, intellect and time. It is quite difficult to establish such relationships when one is busy running the rat race.

A solid I-Thou relationship requires not only a Thou but also an I. The individual needs to have the self-respect and inner strength to be a worthy, sympathetic and loving partner to a Thou. In the It-world of the rat race, though, the individual may also be swept into It-ness.

People may choose shortcuts to winning the attention of others: they play the role of an It. They treat themselves as objects, even though in the depths of their hearts they wish to be treated as subjects. Manifestations of this tendency are ubiquitous. People who dress in a sexually provocative way are presenting themselves as objects. Some will try to catch the attention of others by getting tattooed; piercing their ears, noses, lips, navels, eyelids; dying their hair blue, orange or shocking pink. Some will wear flashy jewelry or speak in a very loud voice. What they are communicating is: notice me, I crave your attention, please don't ignore me. Underlying this non-vocalized plea is the feeling that one will not be noticed unless he is prepared to become an object of attention or unless he conforms to the prevailing fashions, even if those fashions violate his own sense of decency and propriety.

During the summers, we vacation at an ocean resort not far from New York City. Walking on the boardwalk provides a fascinating picture of the It-oriented values of our society. Numerous people run, cycle or walk dressed in tight-fitting spandex shorts. Others wear outfits that seem to have been designed with the specific intention of letting the world know that the wearers have sex organs, a fact we would have assumed anyway. Many beachgoers dress in swimsuits that are ludicrously skimpy, including not a few whose body shapes are not too sleek and svelte. There are, of course, perfectly good, comfortable alternatives to these attention-seeking styles.

These observations are not confined to a summer beach community. They are evident throughout society. The stated and implied message of much of popular culture is: be sexy, be noticed, look young.

Why would people willingly dress in such a way as to make themselves into objects? The answer is that they want to be noticed, admired, longed for. They think that by presenting themselves as Its, they will more likely achieve their goals. They demand less of themselves and of others; no commitment or serious dialogue is invited or expected.

It is easier to give and take a quick thrill than to enter deep and serious I-Thou relationships. This is evidenced not only in the burgeoning pornography business, but in so many of the everyday features of our culture – movies, advertisements, music, fashions. The message is: seize the day, experience or give a thrill, catch the attention of others.

But why would people – who basically want and need I-Thou relationships – behave in such a manner as to promote I-It connections? Why participate in a strategy that is self-destructive, that robs one of dignity and self-respect? Why choose to operate on an artificial, superficial level as a thing?

Human beings all have feelings of insecurity. We need to be needed, appreciated, loved. These tendencies are often exacerbated in teenagers, but continue to exist throughout adult life as well. They manifest themselves in the seemingly opposite characteristics of wanting to conform to a peer group, and wanting to stand out and be noticed. People come to feel that the I-It framework of relationships gives them more immediate "success" in life. They can see themselves as being popular, powerful, unusual, attractive, daring. But underneath the veneer of "success" is the layer of essential insecurity, loneliness and dissatisfaction with self. Exhibitionism may gain the attention of others, but it does not gain their respect and love.

Dr. Norman Lamm, past president of Yeshiva University, has pointed out: "One who lacks the sense of inner dignity and worth will expose himself, as if to say, 'Look at me. Am I not beautiful? Am I not smart? Do you not like me?' The lack of inner dignity leads to exhibitionism, the opposite of modesty, whereas a sense of inner dignity will normally result in the practice of modesty."

Living on an I-It level is a form of escapism. It allows us to avoid considering our lives and relationships with full seriousness. Many people do not want to look in the mirror and see who they really are – the implications of self-knowledge are too overwhelming. So they find escapes: alcohol, drugs, sex, noise, bright lights, raucous music. They spend fortunes of time and money to camouflage themselves, to make themselves artificially appear younger, slimmer, sleeker, richer, more "successful."

Some may retort: "I dress the way I like, and I don't care what anyone else thinks. If I want to have ten rings in my ears and nose, or if I want to have green hair with spikes, or if I want to wear skimpy and tight clothing – that is my business. I don't think these things make me an It. These are my own personal expressions and reflect my freedom to choose."

This line of argumentation, it seems to me, is disingenuous. While such people claim not to care what anyone else thinks, they are consciously dressing in a way that will attract the attention of others. Obviously they do want and expect to be noticed. They consciously or subconsciously want to present themselves as an It. Or they may wish to express defiance of the "establishment." In any case, they see their style of dress as a statement of some sort.

If they genuinely do not care about how their appearance impacts on others, then they are egotists who consider others as Its, as unfeeling things whose opinions are of no consequence. This is not to say that one must be a slave to public opinion – far from it. But one should feel a sensitivity to the feelings of others as a manifestation of simple good manners. Just as it is respectful to eat and drink with good manners, it is respectful to dress with good manners. We are offended by people who eat greedily, who let food drizzle down their chins, and who make all sorts of inappropriate noises. They demonstrate by their behavior that they do not care about our feelings, that we are just objects to them. When people dress disrespectfully, they are behaving similarly. They demonstrate disrespect for themselves and for others. They foster I-It relationships.

It is a matter of simple courtesy and common sense to dress in a nice, respectful and appropriate way. It takes self-respect, and respect for others, to dress as a dignified human being who does not wish to be an object of attention. If you want to be a Thou, then dress as a Thou. If you want others to be Thous, then treat them as Thous.

Engaging in an I-Thou relationship requires depth of feeling and thought. It also demands that one risk giving of him or herself to others, with the possibility of being rejected or betrayed. The more we give of ourselves to others, the greater the possibility of our being let down. Even so, if we do not take the risk of entering into I-Thou relationships, we are condemned to living superficial and unfulfilling lives. If we want to "win" at life, we have to step out of the rat race.

The above discussion has ramifications beyond the interpersonal relationships of individuals. It also relates to inter-group and international relationships. Just as individuals may perceive themselves as struggling in a rat race, so too they may see their groups and nations as being locked into competition with others. The I-It model is at its worst and most dangerous when whole groups or societies engage in negatively stereotyping those whom they view as outsiders or enemies. The victims become caricatures, objects of scorn. Once the dehumanization process begins, it generally leads to oppression, violence and even destruction of the victim.

An example of this phenomenon was the enslavement of black Africans by Christian and Muslim nations. The black slaves were ripped from their social contexts and made to serve masters in settings entirely alien to their traditional ways of life. The Africans may have maintained memories of their home cultures in their minds, but their daily routines were experienced in foreign frameworks. The children and grandchildren of slaves were further removed from the original contexts of their people.

How could one group of human beings treat another group of human beings with such cruelty? The answer is that the dominant group dehumanized the oppressed group. They saw the victims not as human beings like themselves, but as sub-humans, as animals. The African slaves were viewed as objects, as chattel that could be bought and sold. When such an attitude exists, cruelty and violence inevitably follow.

Millions of people throughout history have been dehumanized by their enemies and oppressors. In antiquity, some conquering nations had the policy of depopulating vanquished lands, scattering the population to various locations so that they would lose their group identity. Since the resettled populations did not have enough people to maintain their own way of life, they assimilated into the dominant population and disappeared from history. The victors viewed their victims as things that could be transferred and refashioned. They did not want to recognize their victims as human beings with rights, feelings and their own heritage.

Forced religious conversion is another example of one group trying to impose its ways on another group, within a framework of dehumanization of the victims. Christian missionaries and colonial powers thrived on the idea that they were agents of a superior way of life, that they had the right to subjugate "inferior" peoples. The goal was to "civilize" the natives by breaking them away from their own cultures and assimilating them into Christian, European culture. To "save" souls, they were willing to perpetrate cultural and physical violence against their victims.

The conversionary process, even when well intentioned, entailed a self-righteous cruelty. It was premised on the notion that the missionaries and colonialists had the right to uproot the lives of people, that these victims were merely clay to be molded or smashed.

Tyrants and demagogues throughout the ages have always known the power of stereotyping and dehumanizing target groups or nations. They could whip up the emotions of their followers by depicting victims as hateful, inhuman and savage. Human history is saturated with the blood of innocent victims of hatred and power-lust. Just as the It-world is destructive to interpersonal relationships among individuals, it is even more destructive to relationships among groups and nations.

In his book *Constantine's Sword*, James Carroll offers a serious discussion about the anti-Semitic history of Christianity. He notes how early Christianity, in order to set itself apart from Judaism, created very negative images of Jews and viewed Jews as enemies. Over the ages, these negative stereotypes led to anti-Jewish legislation, persecution, violence and murder. Carroll argues quite intelligently that things did not have to unfold this way. Christianity had other options to foster its own growth; it did not need to demonize Jews. Carroll sees a direct connection between the age-old anti-Jewish teachings of Christianity and the Holocaust. Hitler and his soldiers were Christians – at least in name and upbringing – and they ruthlessly tortured and murdered millions upon millions of innocent people in the cruelest manner. The intellectual dehumanization of Jews led to the mass murder of Jews. For the Nazis and their collaborators, Jews were not considered to be dignified human beings entitled to life.

The dehumanization process is illustrated in a comment by Primo Levi, a prisoner in a Nazi concentration camp. Because he was a chemist, he was given the opportunity to work in a factory. But first, he had to be interviewed by the German doctor in charge. When Primo Levi, the Jewish prisoner, met Dr. Pannwitz, the German authority, Levi was struck by the doctor's manner. The doctor looked at Levi as though he were not also a human being. Levi was pained "because that look was not one between two men; and if I had known how completely to explain the nature of that look, which came as if across the glass window of an aquarium between two beings who live in different worlds, I would also have explained the essence of the great insanity of the third Germany."

Viktor Frankl described a similar sensation. As a Jew in a concentration camp, he was forced to do hard labor. He was once assigned to work on mending a railroad track. The weather was bitter cold and Frankl struggled to keep himself warm. For a moment, he stopped to catch his breath and leaned on his shovel. Just at that moment, a guard saw him and thought him to be loafing on the job. The guard looked at the ragged, emaciated prisoner standing before him. Then, Frankl remembered, "he playfully picked up a stone and threw it at me. That, to me, seemed the way to attract the attention of a beast, to call a domestic animal back to its job, a creature with which you have so little in common that you do not even punish it."

Bruno Bettelheim, who also spent time as a Jewish prisoner in a German concentration camp, noted that the most urgent need of the Jews was to keep remembering that they were still human beings. The Nazis systematically and brutally did everything possible to dehumanize Jews, to treat them as sub-human animals branded with numbers on their arms. By being treated like animals, the fear existed amongst the prisoners that they would come to see themselves as animals, that they would lose all hope. Bettelheim described the concern of the prisoners: "The main problem is to remain alive and unchanged." And, as Bettelheim also noted, "the more absolute the tyranny, the more debilitated the subject."

Rev. Martin Luther King Jr., referring to the evils of segregation of blacks in the United States, underlined the evil of dehumanization of victims. Segregation, he wrote, "distorts the soul and damages the personality. It gives the segregator a false sense of superiority, and the segregated a false sense of inferiority." It results in "relegating persons to the status of things."

As tragic and painful as it is, virtually everyone in the world is a victim of dehumanization. The most obvious victims are persecuted minority groups – religious, racial and national. But the problem is much more universal. White supremacists hate all colored people; black racists preach hatred of all whites. In various countries, anti-American sentiment is cultivated, and terrorists are applauded for attacking American targets or burning American flags. Inter-ethnic and inter-religious battles create new victims every day. Children are raised learning to hate and dehumanize members of different religious, racial and national backgrounds. This hatred is transmitted by the creation of evil stereotypes of target groups in which individuals in these groups are not accorded human qualities.

In describing European attitudes towards the natives in their colonies during the twentieth century, Frantz Fanon stated that the colonialists sought to dehumanize their victims. "The native is declared insensible to ethics; he represents not only the absence of values, but also the negation of values. He is, let us dare to admit, the enemy of values, and in this sense he is the absolute evil. He is the corrosive element, destroying all that comes near him; he is the deforming element, disfiguring all that has to do with beauty or morality; he is the depository of maleficent powers, the unconscious and irretrievable instrument of blind forces." Fanon's words find resonance in the memories of everyone whose group has suffered the indignity of being dehumanized. This means, of course, that it should find resonance in everyone, even members of majority and dominant groups, because such groups are similarly stereotyped by others.

It sometimes happens that the victims of dehumanization become guilty of the same sin. From shame and desperation, they lash out against others whom they perceive as being weaker than they. They think that by tearing down others, they thereby strengthen themselves. This, of course, is false. Their oppression of others is merely a symptom of their own feelings of inferiority.

Demagogues who utilize the rhetoric of hatred are the very worst enemies of human progress and civilization. They sow feelings of malevolence and mistrust into society. They stereotype groups and rob them of their human dignity. The rhetoric of violence and hatred leads to violent and hateful acts. Those who inflict the suffering show themselves to be humanly inferior to their victims.

Sad to say, some of the most vicious demagogues have spewed forth their hatred in the name of God and religion. They have invoked God's name in fanning hatred against those whom they perceive as their enemies. This gross betrayal of the religious message of love and peace has done a great dishonor to both humanity and God.

Victims of dehumanization may also develop inferiority/superiority complexes. They may internalize the hatred aimed against them and come to see themselves as unworthy. They lose their self-respect and come to accept the values and standards of their oppressors. Or, conversely, they may adopt a sense of superiority, attempting to prove that they are better than their detractors. They may come to falsify history in order to create an illustrious past for themselves. In this way, they convince themselves that they are actually superior to those in power.

In recent decades, a tendency has arisen among some group chauvinists to treat history as propaganda. By glorifying their own ethnic history and denigrating the history of others, their goal is ostensibly to build ethnic pride. Yet the ultimate result of this effort must necessarily be negative. Aside from stimulating racial, religious and national antagonisms, it must also inevitably hurt the cause of ethnic history. When group pride is built on delusions and falsifications of history, the result will be a further loss of pride in minority groups, who will eventually realize that they have been duped by fraudulent historians.

People do not need to create false histories in order to have self-respect. Indeed, the first step towards genuine liberation is to transcend the need to prove oneself to be better than others. The values of the rat race keep people struggling against each other, trying to defeat others, hoping to elevate themselves.

The rat race promotes hatred and dehumanization. It contributes to what Erich Fromm has called the "syndrome of decay," that which "prompts men to destroy for the sake of destruction, and to hate for the sake of hate." Because of frustrations, feelings of inferiority and malignant narcissism, many people direct their lives onto the road of hatred and death. Dr. Silvano Arieti has noted that some individuals only feel alive when they are arguing and fighting against something. Such people have psychological problems, often stemming from abnormal relations within their families. People who live according to the syndrome of hatred are at root unhappy people, and they make others quite unhappy too. The problem is that such individuals can only change in a more positive direction if they are ready and willing to take stock of themselves. This process necessitates evaluating the attitudes one has learned at home. One needs the wisdom to accept the values that lead to love and compassion, and the strength to reject the values that lead to hatred and violence.

Many grow up in families and communities that are imbued with hatred and prejudices. They imbibe these negative values with their mothers' milk, so to speak. Their worldview is so dominated by the prejudices they have inherited that they seldom stop to examine these attitudes. They are simply taken as axioms of life.

My maternal grandmother, Sultana Policar Romey, told us of her childhood on the island of Marmara in Turkey. Although the Jewish community there was very small, the Jewish minority generally got along well with the much larger population of Greeks and Turks. But the relative calm that prevailed throughout the year was shattered during Easter week. The Greek Orthodox preachers incited their faithful with hatred against Jews. Drawing on centuries-old anti-Jewish rhetoric and stereotypes, they described the Jews as enemies of Christianity and as murderers. My grandmother told us how the Jewish families of Marmara locked themselves into their homes and boarded up their windows in order to protect themselves from the Christian mob. The Jews lived in terror for the entire week. If a Jewish person happened to be caught outside in the street, Greek gangs would beat him mercilessly.

And then, after Easter week, things returned to "normal." The Greek population calmed down. Jews could once again go about their businesses and resume their daily routines.

This is only one example of how people are raised and trained to hate. There are so many others. Indeed, each of us surely knows someone who has been raised to harbor ill feelings towards members of one group or another. They disdain blacks or whites, Hispanics or Asians, Jews, Catholics or Muslims, or some other group or groups. Since prejudice is so widespread, it is rare to find an individual who has not experienced it.

The test of being a good human being – of rising above the rat race – is in rising above prejudice, replacing the syndrome of decay and hatred with the syndrome of growth and love. I know an individual who had been a devoted member of the Ku Klux Klan in Idaho. He was filled with hatred of blacks, Jews and other groups. Through serious study and reflection, though, he concluded that his life was misdirected. He eventually became a convert to Judaism, practicing this faith with singular piety. He has made it a point to befriend and work with members of those groups that he had been taught to hate. Through a heroic personal effort, he was able to overcome the hatred that his elders had instilled in him; he redirected his life onto a path of growth and love. This man is not alone in having been able to overcome the prejudices with which he grew up. Everyone has the power and the responsibility to adopt an attitude of compassion and love towards others.

Just as individuals who have been raised to hate have been able to overcome hatred, so have victims of hatred been able to overcome the desire for revenge. Great human beings such as Theodor Herzl, Mohandas Ghandi and Martin Luther King Jr., all victims of pathological hatred, were able to rise above their oppressors. Instead of preaching hatred of their enemies, they preached love and peace. They sought to find ways to improve the lot of their people and the lot of humanity in general. They were crushed, but not broken, by the hatred aimed against them. Ultimately, they were victorious in bringing revolutionary progress to their people and the world.

To get out of the rat race, one needs to achieve the realization that it is ultimately unfulfilling and destructive. It does not bring happiness. The forces of unthinking competition and conformity deprive us of personal freedom and autonomy. The I-It orientation of the rat race hinders our development of loving and respectful I-Thou relationships; it also undermines our own human dignity. With the breakdown or absence of the I-Thou framework, the tendencies towards the dehumanization of others increase. Stereotypes and caricatures replace flesh and blood human beings. The syndrome of decay sets in. Words of hatred and disdain give way to acts of cruelty and violence.

"Winning" in the rat race is not a sign of success and happiness. Once we understand this fundamental truth, we can go on to learn how to win at life.

Chapter Five

Starting to Win: Self-Discovery

THE PRESSURES ON US TO LIVE our lives by the rules of the rat race are ubiquitous and powerful. The path of least resistance is simply to go along with the crowd, conforming to popular fashions of thought and behavior. Sometimes, the rat race drives us to behaviors that are hurtful to others and shameful to ourselves. We may feel guilty about betraying our own values, or we might get so involved in the rat race that we come to validate its rules. We become willing participants in the rat race and scorn others who refuse to be drawn in. Like the people in Plato's parable of the cave, we may be so locked into a world of shadows that we resent or persecute those who have seen the world of light.

If we want to win at life, we need to have a clear philosophy that is based on self-respect and respect of others. We need to recognize the rat race as a negative element in human life. It ultimately saps us of our freedom, integrity and ability to relate to others as Thous.

To rise above the rat race, we need a philosophy of life that will include a number of elements. First, we must understand ourselves, our strengths and weaknesses. We must feel connected with our past in particular, and with human history in general. By understanding the traditions in which we were raised, we gain a sense of belonging to a home civilization. Through memories, reminiscences and nostalgic recollections of our past, we see ourselves as part of a historical context. This helps us take a long view of life and not merely react to the pressures of the moment.

Winning at life also requires us to develop the ability to make decisions and to have the inner courage to stand alone, if necessary. Exerting our free will as autonomous human beings is a sine qua non of constructive and responsible living. We need to understand the influences on us from our parents, families, teachers, peers and the surrounding culture at large. Once we can identify the cultural baggage we carry, we can decide how to deal with it. That which is positive, we should integrate into our lives and worldviews. That which is negative and destructive, we need to learn to reject and overcome. We should not want to live in the past, nor should we think that the past is a burden. Responsible living requires finding appropriate balances to the various tensions characteristic of the human predicament. Winning at life entails the development of a philosophy that helps us deal with suffering and death.

Unfortunately, there are no shortcuts or magic formulae that can lift us suddenly and painlessly from the throes of the rat race. We can only succeed if we take the time to think carefully about our lives, and about the ultimate meaning of our lives.

This chapter and those that follow will delineate and explore basic issues that we need to consider if we wish to follow the winning path of life. Unless we ponder these issues, we will find it difficult to distinguish properly between the world of light and the world of shadows, and the claims of the rat race will continue to lure us. These chapters call upon readers to draw from their own experiences and thoughts. This process, since it demands the thoughtful and analytical participation of readers, is in itself an exercise on the winning path of life.

* * *

During the course of a lifetime, a person may wear many masks. In order to curry favor with others, one adopts their attitudes, opinions, styles and behavior patterns. Above all, one wants to belong, to play an acceptable role. At the same time, one also has a separate individual identity within, the hard kernel of one's own being. When one loses sight of his separateness from the masks he wears, he becomes the masks; i.e., a superficial, artificial human being. A person may go through life without examining carefully who he really is. One simply becomes an assortment of ever-changing masks, living life on the surface.

Plato's critique of "the unexamined life" has become something of a cliché, yet the truth that an unexamined life is not worth living remains a startlingly important concept. What is the meaning and purpose of life? What are the ingredients of the entity I call "me"?

How much of "me" is an accumulation of experiences and ideas given to me by others? What is "me" at its core?

Rabbi Aryeh Kaplan, one of the most remarkable Jewish thinkers of the twentieth century, pointed out a profound teaching of the Kabbalists, the devotees of Jewish mystical tradition. In expounding on the real "me," Kabbalists have found a hint in the Hebrew word for "I," *ani*. If the Hebrew letters of *ani* are rearranged, the result is the word *ayn* or *ayin*, which denotes nothingness. The implication is that the real "me" is the nothingness within me.

In this vein, Kabbalists interpret the Biblical verse (Job 28:12) that states: "And wisdom, where is it to be found (*Ve-hahokhmah me-ayin timatsei*)?" The Hebrew words can be read to mean: And wisdom is to be found in nothingness. Until a person can remove all the external masks, can peel off the layers of accumulated borrowings from others – until then he cannot get to the real self. One must descend to the level of "nothingness"; then one may begin to rebuild with the wisdom that has been gained.

The Zohar, the classic text of the Kabbalah, offers an interpretation of Genesis 12:1, where God commands Abram to leave his land, his birthplace, his father's house, to go to a new land to which God will direct him. The Hebrew text reads: "*Lekh lekha*," which is normally translated to mean "get thee out" or "get yourself going." The Zohar notes that the text can also be read more literally as "go to yourself," i.e., to your own self. In order to start off on his new road of life, Abram was told that he first had to go into himself, find out who he was at his core. Once he discovered the "nothingness" within, then he would have the strength and wisdom to confront life in a meaningful and distinctive way.

The "nothingness" at our core develops into a "somethingness" through a variety of processes. Our abilities, talents and powers of observation interact with the world around us. In a sense, our "self" is basically our distinctive way of integrating and harmonizing all the influences on us. The "self" cannot realistically be separated from the influences of others, such as parents, relatives, friends or teachers. It is the task of the "self" to understand, evaluate, accept or reject the external influences on one's life. Optimally, the self's borrowings from others will be positive, constructive and meaningful, helping one on the path to fulfillment and satisfaction. It is axiomatic that in the process of life, the "self" will integrate many influences in an organic way. It is inevitable that the "self" will be covered with external masks.

It is not easy to separate ourselves from our masks. Our self-definition is vastly influenced by the opinions of others. We tend to live up or live down to the evaluations that others make of us. Yet our task is to "know ourselves," to see ourselves as universal and unique individuals, not confused or dominated by definitions of ourselves that are imposed upon us by others.

Much human misery comes as a result of people betraying themselves by adopting artificial personae. They are so dominated by the opinions of others that they govern their lives by those external opinions rather than by what is best and truest for themselves. They present themselves as intellectuals, business tycoons or gregarious show-offs. And yet, deep down they know themselves to be only moderately intelligent and creative; or they detest the world of business competition; or they know themselves to be shy and retiring, preferring quiet conversation in small groups to noisy talk in big crowds.

Yet in order to attain an honest and true self-definition, we need to work at it. We need time to think quietly. We need the ability to view ourselves as objectively as possible, as though we were actually outside of ourselves. We need the strength of character to be able to stand alone and not fear being alone. Only with a calm and strong inner life can we confront the blandishments of the rat race and win by not being lured into its traps. Or, if we have been drawn into it, we need the strength to be able to redirect our lives.

I knew a person in a scientific field who had entered his profession because of parental pressure. He was interested in a literary life; he wanted to read and teach literature. He worked for over twenty years as a scientist, but had the nagging feeling that he had gone down the wrong road. He was not living his own life, but an extension of his parents' lives. He was not being true to his own nature and interests. At last, he gained the courage to quit his job. In spite of serious financial repercussions, he enrolled in graduate school in literature and pursued the advanced degrees he had wanted when he was twenty years younger. His elders were bewildered by his decision. How could he have left a prestigious, high paying position in order to become a financially strapped graduate student? But he had never been happier in his adult life. He had finally reclaimed control over his own life.

Many people second-guess themselves about the roads not taken: What if they had decided differently about their spouse, job, friends, residence, religious commitments, social involvements?

Were these decisions truly their own or were they the result of the wishes and demands of others? While we cannot relive the past, we can learn from it. We can apply lessons from the past to our courses of action in the future.

People are happiest when they respect themselves, when they feel they have taken responsibility for their lives and have done well. Ralph Waldo Emerson wrote that, "There is a time in every man's education when he arrives at the conviction that envy is ignorance; that imitation is suicide; that he must take himself for better and for worse as his portion."

He also proclaimed that, "Whoso would be a man must be a nonconformist." That is, a person who wishes to live life on its deepest level must be able to stand on his or her own, without allowing the attitudes and values of others to supplant personal attitudes and values. In one way or another, everyone wears masks, yet the nonconformist always knows not to confuse the self with the masks.

By nonconformity, I do not mean that a person strives to be different for the sake of standing out. I am speaking, rather, of independence of thought and strength of character. A person may dress in a conventional way and yet be a genuine nonconformist. Indeed, a real nonconformist feels no need to call attention to himself through external trappings. On the other hand, one may dress in an outlandish way and not be a true nonconformist if one dresses that way with the conscious intention of drawing attention to oneself. The unconventional clothing is merely a mask, a come on, a pose. It may reflect inner weakness, exhibitionism and insecurity rather than the poise and self-confidence that are hallmarks of intellectual nonconformity.

A tendency exists among many to present themselves as nonconforming individualists, yet they desperately try to conform to the "nonconformity" of a peer group. A clever cartoon depicts a large group of young people with long hair, pierced ears and noses, wearing baggy clothing. They surround their leader who calls out to them: "Repeat after me: we are individualists; we are nonconformists." The crowd dutifully responds in chorus!

To win at life, one needs to distinguish between genuine selfhood and assumed poses. One needs to be natural, not contrived. Just as the rat race is characterized by frenzied insecurity, a fulfilling life is characterized by calm wisdom and inner poise.

In his book *The Supreme Identity*, Alan Watts described the characteristics of spiritual people. It seems to me that this definition equally applies to all those who are on the winning path of life: "The most spiritual people are the most human. They are natural and easy in manner; they give themselves no airs; they interest themselves in ordinary everyday matters and are not forever talking and thinking about religion. For them there is no difference between spirituality and usual life, and to their awakened insight the lives of the most humdrum and earth-bound people are as much in harmony with the infinite as their own." The type of person Watts describes is a representative example of a nonconformist, in Emerson's sense of the term.

When a person acts in an artificial manner in order to pose as an authentic human being, he is clearly a play actor rather than an approachable Thou. When an artist becomes self-conscious of being an artist, he loses the quality of being a genuine artist. The same is true of a religious personality. An artist, a poet, a religious person is always striving to express some deep feelings or ideas for which his expressions are inadequate. One tries again and again and always, at least to himself, fails. Once one thinks he has succeeded – if only for an instant – in that instant he is no longer an artist, a poet, a religious personality. Vanity has obscured his humility. But it is humility and the sense of inadequacy that serve as the foundation of spiritual greatness.

No two human beings are exactly alike. It is precisely our individualistic worldviews that enable each of us to make a distinctive contribution to society. Our sense of meaning in life is directly correlated with our freedom to participate creatively in the human adventure. Conformity for its own sake and external nonconformity for its own sake are not desiderata; they are trappings of the rat race and they compromise our uniqueness.

The Bible teaches us that God created Adam, starting humanity with one individual. When Adam became aware of his profound loneliness, God created Eve as a separate and unique individual to be his companion. Through them, the human family emerged. The Talmud derives a lesson from the fact that God began humanity with one person rather than creating many people simultaneously, that this demonstrates the value and significance of the individual. Each person is compared to a universe; to destroy one person is to end a universe and to save one life is to save a universe. Like Adam and Eve, each human being is unique and indispensable.

To follow the path of winning at life, we must be keenly aware of our own uniqueness and value, as well as that of others. If we lack self-love and self-respect, we are more likely to join the rat race. We simply do not have the strength to resist the pressures, to stand alone.

Dr. M. Scott Peck has noted that the feeling of being a valuable person is essential to a person's mental health and self-discipline. This feeling derives from parental love. "Such a conviction must be gained in childhood; it is extremely difficult to acquire it during adulthood. Conversely, when children have learned through the love of their parents to feel valuable, it is almost impossible for the vicissitudes of adulthood to destroy their spirit." People who grow up in loving families have the good fortune of experiencing unqualified love and affirmation of their uniqueness.

From parents and elders we first learned what was right and what was wrong – at least what they thought was right and wrong. To the "nothingness" at our cores, we integrated the basic values of our elders. We learned, for example, that we must develop inner strength to deal with life's challenges, to respond to setbacks, to withstand threats. We learned to share, to sense a responsibility for others, to be honest and just and compassionate. If we were very fortunate, we learned the value of being an individual even in a crowd of people, and to value the individual qualities of others. We learned how to argue and how to avoid arguments. We learned that there was a great world of which we were part, and we absorbed the religious teachings and ideals of our elders. We learned to take responsibility.

When we confront moral dilemmas, we draw on the lessons we learned from our parents and elders when we were children. Their moral strengths – and weaknesses – provide a basis for our own responses to the challenges of life. When we do well, we think to ourselves that our parents and elders would be proud of us. When we fail, we may feel that we have not lived up to their expectations of us.

Ideally, parents raise their children to be independent. They nurture and guide and do their best to help their children grow up. They know that the day will come – and should come – when their children will leave home and make their own way in life. The parents' goal is to instill their children with enough knowledge and moral strength to be independent.

Unfortunately, not all parents or elders are successful at conveying a sense of value to their children. Some parents have serious problems of their own and are psychologically, emotionally or morally troubled. Some are controlling and overbearing; they impede the proper development of their offspring. Others have immoral values or warped worldviews imbued with hatred and mistrust. Some simply do not know how to love another because perhaps they themselves were not loved properly by their own parents.

Moreover, even if parents do everything right to convey a sense of value to their children, their children must still face the pressures of the world outside. Parents may tell their children that they are beautiful and good and intelligent, but people outside may convey different messages to them. The child needs to start with a feeling of being loved and honored at home, but this does not necessarily guarantee that he will be immune to the opinions of peers and attitudes of society.

To win at life means that we are involved in an ongoing process of growth and reevaluation. We draw strength from the positive lessons we have learned from our parents and elders, but we always need the clarity of thought and alertness to maintain personal control of our lives. If we fall into unthinking routines and if we accept popular opinions uncritically, then we are in the mode of the rat race. Winning at life entails a commitment to developing one's own uniqueness and to making a distinctive contribution to our world.

My grandfather, Marco Romey, used to say that each person is put on earth to fulfill a specific mission. No one else can fulfill that mission in exactly the same way. Each of us has a unique combination of qualities; no one else has our identical thoughts, feelings, memories and perspective on life. The more one realizes this truth, the more one feels a sense of self-worth and moral responsibility. When a person loses sight of his uniqueness, it is then a natural step to diminish one's sense of personal responsibility.

Many people would rather blend into a crowd than stand out as a distinctive person. Being part of a crowd helps one to shed burdens of personal responsibility, either by saying that he was merely doing what everyone else was doing or that he was only following orders. Self-respect and ongoing self-evaluation are critical aspects of maintaining oneself on the winning road of life.

Erich Fromm has argued that, "authoritarianism in religion and science, let alone politics, is becoming increasingly accepted, not particularly because so many people explicitly believe in it but because they feel themselves individually powerless and anxious."

People lacking the inner strength to be distinctive and morally responsible thereby surrender their personal autonomy to the control of others. In a complex world of billions of people, the individual may have a serious crisis of meaning. If his core personality does not provide self-confidence and uniqueness, it is all too easy to fall under the sway of crowds or charismatic leaders. Conformity relieves one of the responsibility to be unique, to make decisions.

Dr. Silvano Arieti, in his book *The Will to Be Human*, relates an interesting anecdote. In 1922, he was a fourth grader growing up in Italy. At that time, Mussolini was in power and fascism was rapidly becoming the dominant political ideology of the country. Arieti's own teacher was an avid member of the Fascist Party. The pervasive propaganda influenced Arieti, a Jewish child, to write a poem lauding the virtues of fascism. This was before the emergence of the blatantly anti-Jewish features of Italian fascism.

The young Arieti read the poem to his class and was highly praised by his teacher and classmates. Filled with pride, he read the poem that evening to his father. His father, though, was strongly opposed to fascism and scolded his son for having written such a poem. The little boy was stunned. He had received such positive reactions from his teacher and friends, and yet his own father criticized him.

With the passage of years, Arieti came to appreciate his father's wisdom. His own disillusionment with fascism intensified as he contemplated the fascist chants proclaiming that Mussolini was always right, that he could make no mistakes. The young Arieti realized that this ideology was not only false; it was dangerous.

In the late 1930s, Dr. Arieti fled fascist Italy and settled in New York, where he became a prominent psychiatrist. His childhood experiences helped him to understand how human beings internalize external influences.

When we are children, our parents give us commands. Although we lack the experience and wisdom to determine whether these commands are good or bad, we internalize them because they emanate from our parents, whom we trust. As we grow older, the instructions we received from parents and other authority figures become part of our own inner system of self-control. This is a healthy and necessary process, which Dr. Arieti calls "endocracy." Endocracy means that we have learned the basic rules of our civilization and have willingly incorporated them into our own systems of life.

Dr. Arieti also writes of endocratic surplus. This occurs when we internalize too much from external sources, thus losing our autonomy. We judge and act according to prevailing values or influences imposed upon us by others. Throughout history, people have been victims of endocratic surplus when they have uncritically absorbed dangerous ideologies, without having freely evaluated what they were absorbing. This is how the child Arieti had become enamored with fascism under the influence of his teacher.

A century and a half ago, many Americans were proponents of slavery – not because they were innately bad people, but because they were raised to think that slavery was a natural and morally acceptable system. Indeed, throughout history, people have believed absurd and dangerous things because they did not have the inner strength and clarity to reject prevailing attitudes. Endocratic surplus is not something that existed only in past eras, but continues to be a factor in all of our lives. Individuals absorb prejudices and false assumptions from their family, peers and general culture.

The more endocratic surplus we have, the less free we are. We diminish our ability to think critically; we live according to the thoughts and emotions projected into us by others. To be spiritually healthy human beings, we need to maintain a proper balance. We must recognize those concepts and rules that have been internalized to our benefit and with our ultimate approval, and we must also be able to identify endocratic surplus which deprives us of our freedom and autonomy.

We all necessarily learn from others. Civilization depends on the orderly communication and transmission of modes of thinking and behaving. We depend on the authority of others for many things. Yet, genuine authority must be authoritative – not authoritarian. A person gains authority with us by winning our respect and trust. An authoritarian approach, though, threatens mature, free human life. While authoritativeness fosters a healthy endocracy, authoritarianism often engenders an unhealthy endocratic surplus.

One of the perennial problems confronting humanity is the emergence of authoritarian figures who gain sway over others. Authoritarians, whether they be low-grade bullies, cult leaders or tyrants, are classic examples of individuals who view other human beings as Its. By exploiting and manipulating others, these authoritarian types attempt to satisfy their inner needs to exert power or gain prominence. Dr. Arieti has suggested that the search for power by authoritarian personalities "is a reaction to a double set of anxieties: anxiety caused by fear of others, and anxiety caused by dissatisfaction about oneself." Such people compensate for their own inadequacies by seeking to have power over others. If others bend to their will, they feel validated. If deprived of power, they feel empty and forlorn. Such people have a weak inner core; they are unfulfilled human beings, and they are dangerous. They thrive on the subservience of others. They create scapegoats upon whom they can direct their destructive energies.

The New York Times (Sunday, May 20, 2001) printed an article about the phenomenon of bullying. It referred to a study by researchers from York University who studied videotapes of fifty-three episodes of bullying among elementary school students on school playgrounds. They found that fifty-four percent of the time, onlookers stood by passively when the bully attacked the victim. The silence of the onlookers, of course, results in reinforcing the bully's behavior. Twenty-one percent of the time, some onlookers actually joined the bully in taunting the victim. Perhaps they hoped to win approval from the bully, or at least avoid becoming a victim in the future. In only twenty-five percent of the cases did a child attempt to help the victim by stepping in or calling a teacher for help.

Bullies grow in their influence because others are prepared to go along with them, or at least do not resist them. Bullying, obviously, is not merely symptomatic of school children, but is a feature of adult society as well. It also manifests itself in the relationships between groups and nations. But it is important to remember that bullies, cult leaders and tyrants could not exert authority if everyone else resisted them. The "success" of such personalities is made possible by the active or passive collaboration of others.

The authoritarians see life as a rat race; they are prepared to do whatever is necessary to advance themselves, to get ahead. When others accept this worldview without resistance, they enable the authoritarians to gain power. So much of human history has been dominated by this pattern; we have suffered an endless parade of wars, persecutions, genocides. The authoritarians could not do these things on their own; they have always required and depended on an army of followers who did not challenge their leadership or were too fearful to do so. Strong tyrants depend on weak masses.

Authoritarians do not wish to see others as fellow human beings with unique and distinctive qualities. They are not interested in – and in fact very much oppose – freedom of expression, intellectual inquiry and dissent. To achieve their goals, they feel they need to quash all opposition. The great American jurist, Learned Hand, wrote: "That community is already in the process of dissolution, where each man begins to eye his neighbor as a possible enemy, where nonconformity with the accepted creed is a mark of disaffection; where denunciation takes the place of evidence; where orthodoxy chokes freedom of dissent. Those who begin coercive elimination of dissent, soon find themselves exterminating

dissenters. Compulsory unification of opinion achieves only the unanimity of the graveyard."

Winning at life requires a clear rejection of the rules of the rat race. It demands that each individual go to his own core of being, strengthen his inner life and moral courage, and remain a thinking nonconformist, independent and free. It requires a constant evaluation and reevaluation of prevailing attitudes, as well as a commitment to reject authoritarianism. It demands that we view life not as a frenzied, dangerous competition, but as a framework for working in harmony with others, seeing the uniqueness of each individual and trying to see the other as a Thou.

Chapter Six

Memories: Providing Context for Our Lives

As was discussed earlier, winning at life requires self-knowledge; the ability to distinguish between our real selves and the external definitions of ourselves projected onto us by others. But when we try to understand ourselves, we come to realize just how complex we are. Human beings are composed of so many elements. We are shaped by our genetic make-ups, our upbringings, our teachers and peers, the values of general society, our experiences, our intellectual, physical and emotional constitutions.

So many influences help shape who we are. How we understand and integrate these influences helps define our personalities and distinctive worldviews. We need calmness of mind and patience of spirit to achieve a high degree of self-understanding.

One of the features of modern society, though, is that we often feel that we are overly busy, pressured and torn by conflicting interests. The novelist Italo Calvino has noted that, "we are bombarded today by such a quantity of images that we can no longer distinguish direct experience from what we have seen for a few seconds on television. The memory is littered with bits and pieces of images, like a rubbish dump, and it is more and more unlikely that any one form among so many will succeed in standing out."

What Calvino was observing is a problematic feature of modernity – the quick pace of life. We live in a world of immediacy. We are barraged with all sorts of information, instantly. Radio, television, the internet, cell phones and beepers are ubiquitous. We are constantly on call. We always seem to be in a rush or in need of immediate attention. Indeed, one of the recurring phrases in popular advertising is "immediate relief." From instant coffee to instant lotto cash to instant gratification, moderns want shortcuts – the quickest way to get from point A to point B – and with the least effort and personal commitment.

A corollary of the stress on immediacy is the development of a short-term view of life. We go from moment to moment, from crisis to crisis. We place less emphasis on contemplating the past or planning long-range for the future.

One September morning, I was walking along the seashore contemplating ideas for a book I was then working on. The summer beach season was over and very few people were around. In the distance, though, I detected someone who appeared to be busy building an elaborate sand castle. As I came closer, I saw that the industrious builder was a gray-haired man. He worked with childlike intensity, creating a sand castle that would soon be flattened by the incoming tide.

My first assumption was that he was working on this sand castle together with his children or grandchildren. I looked around but saw no children nearby. The man, who appeared to me to be in his fifties, was doing this project by himself.

I pondered the situation. What did this man have in mind? He was certainly no longer a child, so why was he engaging in child's play? Why was he working so intensely on a sand castle, knowing full well that it would soon be overrun by the ocean's waves?

I thought: This gray-haired man, at this particular moment, has cast himself back into his past. He is a middle-aged man and he is a child – both at the same time. He has come to the beach to play in the sand, as he must have done when he was a child. Perhaps he imagines those early times in his life when he came to the beach with his parents and family. Perhaps digging in the sand helps him retrieve those simpler times. He builds a sand castle that will soon perish, but isn't that merely a parable for all of life? Doesn't everything we build in our lives ultimately end up swallowed by the ocean of time? A hundred years from now, a thousand years from now, will there be even the slightest trace on earth of our existence, of our struggles and achievements?

If the man had permanently reverted to reveries of childhood, he would be a troubled human being. He would be engaging in escapism, in fantasy. He would have been avoiding present responsibility by dreaming that he was still dwelling in the past. But more likely, he was merely engaging in temporary daydreaming. He was taking a short break from his stress-filled life, trying to reconnect with the quiet, peace and happiness of his past. His building of the sand castle, far from being a sign of regressive development, may actually have been a way for him to clear his mind so that he could focus again on taking control of his life.

Human life operates on different levels, often simultaneously. We may be thinking one thing, saying another, feeling yet something else. In order to understand ourselves, we need to be able to take breaks from the routine of life, to think quietly, to reminisce, to build sand castles. Good memories from our past can give us moments of pleasure as well as keep us linked to our past.

Our family was recently watching old home movies taken in the mid-1950s. On the screen, I saw my parents, grandparents, uncles and aunts, almost all of whom are now deceased. My siblings, cousins and I were little children in the movies.

The old films showed us all singing, dancing, celebrating happy events in our lives. I felt a strange poignancy in seeing images of my parents in the movies, depicting a time when they were younger than I am now.

Viewing old movies or looking over old photographs can be a seemingly surrealistic experience. We have the odd sense of being in two places and in two different eras at the same moment. We live now, yet we seem to experience being in the realm of the pictures as well. This sensation awakens within us our relationships and connections with the past.

In 1952, the neurologist Dr. Wilder Penfield published an important study on the nature of human memory. He discussed three aspects of memory. First, our brains record every experience we have. Without this ability to store information, memory could not function. Second, we have the capacity to retrieve information from our memory bank. Sometimes we can recall data more efficiently and sometimes less efficiently. Yet if we lacked the ability to retrieve information altogether, we would be seriously handicapped. Our senses of identity would be destroyed; it is memory that maintains the integrity of our senses of self. If we are separated from our pasts, we essentially are separated from our own cohesive identities. Paul Davies, a thoughtful modern philosopher of science, has pointed out that, "our conception of ourselves is strongly rooted in our memory of past experiences. It is not at all clear that, in the absence of memory, the self would retain any meaning whatever." It is essentially through the power of memory that we recognize ourselves to be the same individual from day to day.

Dr. Penfield noted that a third quality of memory is the ability to re-enter the past on an emotional level. When people remember certain experiences, they also revive the actual feelings and sensations that accompanied those experiences when they originally occurred. For example, the fragrance of freshly baked bread might transport us into a world of memories and feelings relating to our mother's kitchen. Hearing a certain melody might evoke emotions we felt when we heard that melody at a party we attended as teenagers. Memories can trigger within us a profound sense of nostalgia, of reliving past times. If only for an instant, we find ourselves transported back in time. We can smell the fragrances, hear the voices, hold the hands.

Our memories of the past help define who we are. Reminiscing is an important part of our psychological development and can serve as the foundation of a mature historical sense. The universe did not start with us. We have family histories, ancestors whose voices in some way still speak to us and through us. We are connected to various traditions – religious, national and cultural. Innumerable generations preceded us, bequeathing patterns of living, thinking, creating, expressing. Each human being is born into a historical context and is shaped by the society in which he was raised. It is precisely the sense of rootedness in tradition that can anchor us so that we can be creative and free. Without that anchor, people may drift from one direction to another, forever searching for the elusive "truth." They follow spiritual fads, they have difficulty making genuine commitments, they feel rootless.

It is natural to gain inner strength and security from the familiar framework of the civilization in which we developed. We seek meaning in the personalities, places and events of earlier times. Many are fascinated by their family genealogies. They search for their family roots, eager to push their family history as far back as possible. Some do extensive research; others go to significant expense to hire genealogists who will trace back their family trees. Even those with a negligible interest in genealogy are interested to learn information about their family history.

Almost everyone is interested in family stories told by their parents, grandparents and elder relatives. These stories open a distant world, describing past times. They link us with a past that belongs to us, that stands as the foundation of our own lives.

We need to listen to the voices of our earlier generations and recognize our connections with our family traditions. In so doing, we actually foster our own individuality. We are not merely borrowers from the previous generations; we are contributors to the future generations. We each have something unique to add to the history of our family and to the history of humanity.

A nineteenth-century poet, Solomon Frug, wrote a poem entitled *The Daughter of the Sexton*. It recounts the story of a venerable rabbi who was very ill, nearing death. Community leaders, not wanting the sage to die, decided to ask the rabbi's followers to donate a part of their own allotted years to the rabbi. Thus, if each person were to contribute a few weeks or months of his life to the rabbi, then the rabbi's life would be prolonged.

The sexton of the synagogue was given the responsibility of collecting the "donations." Individuals told him the amount of time they were willing to have deducted from their lives and to be applied to the account of the rabbi. When the sexton came to his own home, his daughter answered the door. She was so distressed by the rabbi's plight that she told her father that she wished to donate her entire life to the rabbi. The sexton was frantic – but it was too late. The contribution had been offered freely and now it had to be paid.

The sexton's daughter died and the rabbi recovered his health. He continued to live the years that had been donated to him by the sexton's daughter. Years later, the rabbi heard a voice in his head – it was the voice of the sexton's daughter at the wedding she had never had, her cries during the childbirth of children she had never bore. And then he heard the voice of her death groans, and the rabbi died.

This poignant tale suggests a powerful truth of human experience: our lives are intertwined with the lives of others. Our personalities have a specific core, but are also an amalgam of the relationships we have had with others. People "donate" part of their lives to us, just as we constantly "donate" part of our lives to them. Symbolically, each human life is composed of donations from the lives of others and each human being donates some of his time allotment to others.

As the rabbi in Frug's poem heard the voice of the sexton's daughter, each person hears the voices of those who have contributed to one's life. These voices, including those of loved ones who have died, continue to be heard by us as long as we live.

The "donations" we have received from parents, grandparents, uncles and aunts are important elements in our inner lives. Optimally, they form the bedrock of our sense of rootedness in the world. We derive much from the inherited wisdom and experience of past generations. In some profound way, we continue to hear their voices throughout our lives.

As we grow older, we tend to think back on the days of childhood. Things that seemed commonplace or insignificant then, now strike us as being unique and special. We remember people, events, mannerisms, songs, foods. We see significance in them for our lives and for the lives of our families.

We become more aware of the voices of the past generations of loved ones. We enjoy recounting stories about them. We find ourselves quoting their words of advice, their witticisms and their jokes. We sometimes see people who resemble them in some feature or mannerism, and the gates of our memories and feelings are opened wide. It sometimes happens that we start to see in ourselves various traits of our deceased loved ones: a gesture, a way of thinking, a style of laughing or crying. With the passing of time, we may even tend to judge their foibles more charitably. Traits that had bothered us while they were alive now can be looked at with a sense of humor and forgiveness.

We are, of course, very different people from who they were. Yet they have donated much of their lives to us. Our lives are significantly influenced by their "donations" to us.

The noted psychiatrist, Dr. S. Ferenczi, wrote that, "in our innermost soul we are still children, and we remain so throughout life." He pointed out that we always need authority figures, such as parents, who will offer us guidance and reassurance. In the absence of parents, we seek out other authority figures, such as elder relatives, clergy and teachers. When the authority figures are not immediately available, our minds conjure them up and they continue to influence us through our memories of them.

Memories of childhood come to mind especially when we visit places that played significant roles in our early lives. We remember so many details about the places and the people of those bygone days.

In the 1840s, Abraham Lincoln revisited his old neighborhood in Indiana where he had spent part of his childhood, and where his mother had died. In returning to his old home, he was confronted with mixed emotions and he expressed his feelings in a poem:

> My childhood's home I see again
> And sadden with the view;
> And still, as mem'ries crowd my brain,
> There's pleasure in it too.

It is sad to go home again after so many years and to find that you are something of a stranger there. This is where you used to belong; this is where you spent much precious time; this is a source of lifelong memories and emotions. But your time there has passed. You can only relate to your old home through the power of memory.

Lincoln noted, though, that the sad feelings of returning home are mixed with pleasure as well. The very confrontation with old familiar places evokes happy thoughts and feelings. One feels in some way transported back to those bygone days when one lived there. The vivid memories reawaken past experiences. You smell the fresh-cut grass and you are a child again. It is as though you can feel your father's hand holding yours, your mother's hand brushing your hair off your forehead.

Daniel Webster, like Lincoln, waxed nostalgic when returning to the humble home of his childhood in New Hampshire. Although he had grown into a prominent and powerful political figure, Webster retained strong emotional connections with his birthplace. In one of his speeches, he informed his audience that the remains of his old house in New Hampshire still exist. "I make to it an annual visit. I carry my children to it, to teach them the hardship endured by the generations which have gone before them. I love to dwell on the tender recollections, the kindred ties, the early affections, and the touching narratives and incidents, which mingle with all I know of this primitive abode."

Rabbi Joseph B. Soloveitchik, one of the leading religious thinkers of the twentieth century, delivered a lecture on the anniversary of the death of his father. He remarked: "It seems to me as if my father were yet alive, although four years have come and gone since his death. It is in a qualitative sense that I experience his nearness and spirit tonight. I cannot explain the... spiritual picture of my father that hovers near me tonight, as in yesteryear of physical existence.... Our sages have said... 'the righteous are exalted in death more than in life.' If time be measured qualitatively, we may understand how their influence lingers on after their death and why the past is eternally bound with the present."

In pondering the lives of loved ones of the past generations, we do not simply remember the mundane details of their lives. Rather, we tend to consider their lives more meditatively; we think about their ideas, aspirations, achievements and failures. Indeed, once they have died and are no longer a physical presence in our lives, we begin to understand their lives on a deeper, more qualitative level. If we cannot hear their voices or feel their hugs, we can contemplate their lives and reflect on what we learned from them. The more we feel connected with our forebears, the more we feel strong and free, universal and unique.

My mother, Rachel Romey Angel, died in May 1983 after a long battle with cancer. Being a rabbi, I officiated at her funeral. During the eulogy, the thought occurred to me: "I am an orphan."

The phrase struck me as odd, even as I first thought and uttered it. At the time, I was nearly thirty-eight years old, married, with children of my own. I was reasonably successful in my professional and personal life. I was not helpless or lost – and yet I felt orphaned.

In July 1991, my father, Victor B. Angel, died. This made my "orphanhood" complete. There were no more parents to turn to, no more unqualified love that only a parent can give, no mother or father with whom to share life's important moments.

In my book *The Orphaned Adult*, I concluded the first chapter with the following observation: "Adult orphans, being adults, bring reason, experience and strength to their confrontation with this life crisis. Adult orphans, being orphans, bring anxiety, emotional conflict and weakness to this life crisis. Adult orphans are wise and ignorant, strong and weak, courageous and frightened. We are a society of orphans."

A story is told of Rabbi Abraham Isaac Kook, one of the great Jewish thinkers and mystics of the twentieth century. His widowed mother lived to a ripe old age. When she died, Rabbi Kook grieved bitterly over her demise. His students were taken aback by their teacher's behavior. They asked him: "Why do you cry so mournfully? After all, your mother was quite elderly. No one lives forever. Certainly you could not have expected her to go on living indefinitely." Rabbi Kook nodded his head. "Yes," he told his students, "of course I know these things. Why then do I cry at the death of my mother? I cry because there is no one left in the world who can call me 'my son.'"

In the normal course of events, we reach the point in life when we are orphaned of our parents and their generation. We find that we *are* the new elders. A generation has come, a generation has gone – and we stand at the brink. We may return to our home-towns, the cemetery where our parents are buried, the old neighborhoods where we spent our childhoods. We know, deep in our souls, that a void has opened in our lives. When we reach this stage of life, we often find ourselves looking back so that we will gain the strength to look ahead.

The psychiatrist and philosopher, Viktor Frankl, has suggested that the truest and surest aspects of life are in the past. They have already been lived; they are done and can never be changed. While the future is uncertain, the past is safe. The older one grows, the more of one's life has been deposited in the secure and eternal treasury of history. Being an elder, then, has its genuine satisfactions.

Memory is personal, even subjective. Through the prism of memory, the past may be glorified or demonized, depending on what we choose to remember and what we choose to forget. A strong tendency exists, though, to idealize the good old days. Why do we do this? Perhaps it reflects a wishful idealism; we want to believe in the goodness of humanity. When we contemplate the present, we often see human flaws – greed, selfishness, hatred and violence. Since the world we live in is far from ideal, we place the golden age safely in the past. There was a better time, there were better people, and there were greater leaders – in the past.

Through memories, we may find ourselves longing for the sense of security, stability and traditionalism that we think characterized earlier times. Those were the days when children listened to parents, when parents were faithful to the traditions of their parents, when families were whole, when people felt that they belonged to a community. In spite of material and spiritual shortcomings that certainly existed in those days, we derive inspiration and inner strength from our idealization of the best things that we experienced: love, respect, family solidarity, a clear value system, a sense of belonging.

Emily Dickinson wrote: "Home is the definition of God." As God gives meaning and orderliness to the universe, so, too, a home imbues the individual with a unique way of making sense of life. Our sense of home gives us the inner strength to confront crises and disruptions. Home is not essentially a physical place. Rather it is all the memories and associations that go with it. It is a state of mind – ultimately the bedrock of our personalities.

A healthy nostalgia for home is a source of both strength and pleasure. But nostalgia can also be overdone and can serve as a means of escape from the everyday challenges of life. For all its importance as the foundation of our lives, we do not live in the past. We may have the deepest feelings of respect, reverence and nostalgia for olden times, but we live in the present and must move onward. A visit to the cemetery or a look through old photograph albums reminds us that the past has a powerful hold on us, yet it is not the only key to our lives.

A Persian tale tells of a poor young man who was walking down the street feeling sorry for himself. Unexpectedly, he met an elderly sage who made a remarkable offer. The wise man invited him to come and live with him and some colleagues in a palace. The young man would be able to live comfortably, without having to worry any longer about poverty.

The young man readily accepted the invitation. When they arrived at the palace, the youth was impressed with the beauty of the premises and looked forward to living a life of opulence. However, he noticed that the elderly sage and his colleagues appeared to be deeply sad. He could not understand why they were morose, seeing that they lived in such excellent circumstances. When he asked his mentor why the residents were so sad, the elder simply nodded his head without offering an explanation.

The elder told the youth that he could enjoy all that was in the palace. He then showed him a large door and said: "You have free use of the entire palace, but it is forbidden to open this door. Except for this prohibition, everything is accessible to you."

As time passed, the young man became more and more curious to learn what was behind that door. But he remembered the instructions of his mentor and refrained from opening it. Meanwhile, the various old men who lived in the palace were dying off. Finally, only the elderly sage and the young man remained. The old sage said: "I will die soon, and then this palace will become yours. You will be able to live your entire life here in comfort. You will be a wealthy man. But remember, do not open the forbidden door." Not long afterward, the elderly man died.

The young man grieved the loss of his master. But now he had a nagging desire to see what was behind the forbidden door. He reasoned: If I have become master of this palace, why shouldn't I know what is behind the door? What was the elder hiding from me?

One day, the young man decided to defy his master's instructions. He opened the door and found that it led to a long, dark road. He entered and began walking. At last he came to an opening and found himself in a wonderful place, drenched with light and beauty. People greeted him with great respect. He was immediately led to a magnificent palace that was given to him. He was granted the best of everything. He had a beautiful wife, wonderful friends, an abundance of all good things. He had never been more content. He imagined that it was impossible for a human being to be happier than he was. He became angry with his former mentor for having tried to deprive him of this happy destination.

As time passed, his friends and advisers told him that they were glad he was living among them. But they gave him one warning. In his palace was a door that was never to be opened. As long as he did not open the door, he would be able to remain in this idyllic world.

Time passed. The mystery of the door gnawed at him. Perhaps they had warned him not to open it because it led to an even more exquisite world. After all, he had defied his mentor and was rewarded by finding this blissful place. If he were to go through this door, he might find yet more blessings and happiness.

He went to the forbidden door and opened it. Behind it was a long, dark path. He entered and began walking. Soon he found himself back in the palace that his mentor had given to him. The door slammed shut, leaving him in the palace. His heart leaped with despair. He struggled to open the door so that he could return to the wonderful world that he had left. The door would not open again for him. He could never return to his former happiness. He was filled with melancholy. His face grew sad. Now he understood the sadness of the elderly sage and his colleagues.

This parable – similar to the Garden of Eden story – tells of a lost, golden age, of a past glory that can never again be retrieved.

We had something special; we lost it; we cannot go back. The sadness persists, coloring the rest of our lives.

The sadness often manifests itself as nostalgia. We long for the good old days, the days of our youth, the days of our happiness. Or we long for a past era when people were better, more heroic and righteous. As long as these feelings do not dominate our personalities, they provide a certain bittersweet wisdom. If they lead one to disparage life as it is and yearn to live in the past, they can be destructive. It is possible to be dissatisfied with the present; it is not possible to live in the past.

John Steinbeck's short story, *A Leader of the People*, provides a moving illustration of a man who very much wanted to live in the past, who never made peace with the present. In his earlier days, he had led a wagon train across the United States. It was a rugged and dangerous adventure, calling on him and his followers to put up with many hardships and threats of attacks by Indians. When he successfully brought his group into California, there was great rejoicing. The man was elated at having accomplished such a marvelous achievement.

That adventure, though, became the focus of his life. He always thought back on the various incidents and challenges of the cross-country trip. Nothing in his later life could compare with the excitement of his leading that wagon train. When he visited his daughter and her family, he told story after story about his adventures. His son-in-law grew sick and tired of the stories — didn't the old man realize that he was a bore, that they had already heard his stories dozens of times? His daughter, with great sympathy for her father, reminded her husband of her father's situation. He had once done something great – that adventure was the crowning achievement of his life – and he never got past it. He must have cried when he saw the Pacific Ocean, knowing that the trip had come to an end, that there was no more frontier to cross. He wanted that trip to go on and on, never to end. But it did end. The only way he could keep it going was through his memories, and through his telling stories about the good old days. The old man, who had once done something extraordinary, had become a pitiable and even tragic character because the focus of his life was in the past.

On some level, though, all people have a desire to live in the past. Don Quixote dreamed of a bygone era of chivalry, when men were noble and women were pure and fair. He wanted to be part of the heroic world of knights and ladies. The real world in which he lived was vulgar, cruel and sordid. He found a better reality in the romantic novels describing the lives of chivalrous knights, and he chose to live as a knight. Surely, Don Quixote was mad. But doesn't his madness resonate in many thoughtful people? Wouldn't we prefer to live a life dedicated to Truth, Virtue and Honor? Don't we respect the deeply felt need to fight for the right, against all foes and in spite of all odds? Don Quixote was mad. In losing touch with reality, he transferred himself into a world of fantasy. Yet I suppose that all great humans – probably all good humans – have something of Don Quixote within them.

Winning at life involves having a healthy, comfortable relation-ship with one's past, and with history in general. To reminisce and idealize the past too much is a sign of escapism. But brushing aside or ignoring the claims of the past are signs of the rat race.

For many people, the past is not viewed as a time of goodness and security. Especially for those who grew up in violent or troubled homes, the memories of the past evoke painful feelings. Just as some imagine the past in larger-than-life joy and brightness, others imagine the past in larger-than-life horror and darkness. Those with negative views of the past may find themselves psychologically at war with their parents and all they represent.

Some years ago, I counseled a woman whose mother had recently died. The daughter, then in her mid-forties, had had a troubled relationship with her mother. The mother criticized her constantly, making her feel guilty and unworthy. Although the daughter had spent a lifetime trying to win her mother's approval, she never succeeded. Indeed, even on her deathbed, the mother had nasty things to say to her daughter, telling her that she had made a mess of her life and that she had not lived up to her mother's expectations.

The daughter came to me because she had conflicted feelings towards her mother. On the one hand, she knew she was supposed to respect her and therefore felt guilty about her negative feelings about her. On the other hand, she was angry at the way her mother had treated her. She was especially bitter that her mother could find nothing nice to say even at the very end of her life.

Parents are supposed to give their children a sense of self-worth and self-confidence. Parents who tear their children down commit a serious error. Often enough, destructive parents were themselves raised by destructive parents; they perpetuate the damaging parent-child pattern that they themselves experienced as children. This was the case with the mother of the daughter who had come to me for counseling. She was guilty of bad parenting, but was only doing to her daughter what her parents had done to her. She had not had the inner strength or wisdom to break the negative cycle. Thus, she lived her life at odds with her own parents and then succeeded in alienating her own children. When she died, she left this world profoundly alone and bitter.

Once the daughter came to see the truth of this observation, she also came to realize that she had to break the negative patterns of the previous generations of her family. She needed to focus on her own strengths, to forge a positive and constructive relationship with her own offspring. She learned to draw on the good memories she had of her mother – as for the many bad memories, she learned to overcome them.

Quite a few people suffer their entire lifetimes from negative baggage with which they were burdened from childhood. Their parents, relatives and teachers were inadequate in their responsibilities. Profound emotional scars may be apparent in those who grew up in broken or troubled homes, in unloving and unaffirming environments. The problem is that such individuals may pass on these same problems to their own children. Having grown up without the wholeness of a loving family, they may come to assume that this is the way life necessarily has to be.

For such people, it is particularly important to establish an honest relationship with the past. When negative features of the past impinge on their lives, they need to be clear-headed enough to overcome the destructive patterns. Human beings are not irrevocably programmed by their parents, grandparents, relatives and teachers. Honesty and clarity can help us to identify problem areas; courage and strength of character can help us overcome them.

The words of parents and teachers, because they are so authoritative to children, carry great weight. How many people have grown up thinking they were stupid or clumsy or ugly because authority figures had so characterized them? How many people have grown up knowing that they were intelligent, good-looking and talented, but still felt that they somehow did not meet the higher standards that authority figures had set for them? Such people, though quite capable, have the constant feeling of being unworthy and inadequate. Unless they can overcome the negative memories and influences of the past, their self-images will remain badly tarnished.

The psychiatrist, Arno Gruen, has written of what he calls the "betrayal of the self." We betray ourselves when we try to live up to false and unrealistic standards, when we do not have a clear and honest sense of ourselves. "Thus, it is our compulsion to fit an image of power which keeps us from experiencing the reality that is – with devastating consequences! We establish irrational ideals of the 'real' man and the 'right kind' of woman, which not only separate us more and more from our genuine potentialities, but in the long run also lead us into self-destructiveness."

On a number of occasions, I have counseled individuals whose self-rage and frustration had not diminished, even years after the deaths of their parents. I asked them: Do you think that your parents would want you to torment yourself? Would they want you to carry on the negative patterns which you learned from them, even though these patterns are damaging to you and to your relationships with your loved ones? Or do you think they would be able to realize that they had made serious mistakes in their relationship with you, mistakes that their own parents might have made with them? Wouldn't they feel contrite that they have caused you so much grief, and wouldn't they want you to move ahead with your life in a positive, happy and loving way? Don't you think your parents' love was great enough to want you to be able to live a meaningful and satisfying life?

If people can recognize their parents' shortcomings and forgive them, they can begin the process of healing. If they believe that their parents truly loved them and would want them to live happily with self-esteem, then they can get past their past. They can continue to love their parents for all the good they did, but they can now work to undo the effects of negative qualities that their parents had demonstrated.

But, if they believe that their parents really were cruel, unloving people, then why should they allow the influences of those bad parents to continue to hurt them? Why not simply say: My parents, for whatever reasons, were not good parents; they wished me ill and did me harm. I have no obligation to internalize the destructive messages they have imposed upon me. On the contrary, I have an obligation to live a good and meaningful life in spite of having had bad parents.

Winning at life entails not only reconciliation with our past, but also a clear recognition that we have the power to change. We are in control of our lives. We can sift out negative influences and redirect ourselves.

Memories provide us with a context for our lives; they connect us to our past and remind us of the generations that have come before us. When the memories are positive, they strengthen us. When they are negative, they challenge us to overcome the bad influences they conjure up within us. If we drift too much into a life of memory and nostalgia, we sink into a form of escapism. But if we don't make time for memories and nostalgia, we sink deeper into the rat race.

Chapter Seven

Making Decisions and Taking Responsibility

MARGARET MEAD DESCRIBED modern western culture as "prefigurative." This is a condition where authority does not reside with the elders, as in traditional cultures; nor with peers, as in cofigurative cultures. Rather, we live in a setting where all authority has been shaken. No one, not the elders and not the younger generation, can say with certainty what the future will bring. Our age is one of incredible technological advances – life changes from day to day. How can elders, or even peers, give authoritative and reliable advice about a world that changes with such rapidity?

Mead has written: "In the past there were always some elders who knew more than any children in terms of their experience of having grown up within a cultural system. Today there are none. It is not only that parents are no longer guides, but that there are no guides, whether one seeks them in one's country or abroad." She further noted that our modern situation manifests itself as a crisis of faith in religion, political ideology and science. People feel deprived of sources of security.

Mead views moderns as pioneers in a new frontier. The authorities of the past are inadequate to prepare us for the challenges we face. Our basic sense of security and social stability is threatened, and we have no time-tested answers to apply to our new dilemma. The modern era is characterized by fear of weapons of mass destruction, major threats to the earth's environment, and questions of the ultimate meaning and purpose of life.

Prefigurative culture places a greater burden on individuals to take responsibility for themselves and for their futures. It wants children to grow "straight and tall, into a future that must be left open and free."

Of course, Mead understands that human nature is not new; the advance in human knowledge is not new; the search for truth and meaning is not new. Without connection to our historic roots, the new branches on the tree of human civilization will wither. Yet she touches on a prevailing feeling among moderns that our condition is somehow unprecedented. In some ways, it surely is.

Peter Berger, the eminent sociologist of religion, has used the phrase "the homeless mind" to describe what he views as a peculiar problem of moderns. Throughout most of human history, people lived in social settings that were basically unified. They had religious beliefs and traditions that gave meaning and orderliness to their lives. Individuals had a "home world," a meaningful center of life. In modern times, however, the home world has become vastly weakened. We confront a plurality of lifestyles, ideals and beliefs. Our own basic values are challenged, modified, weakened.

Berger has argued that moderns have suffered from a deepening condition of "homelessness." In being so receptive to outside influences, people have compromised their ability to maintain the structure of their own home world. The outside world spills in and overwhelms.

The past several centuries have been marked by phenomenal advances in technology and communications. Stable, traditional cultures have been disintegrating worldwide. Millions of people have moved from their original homes, have given up or watered down their traditional cultural and religious patterns, have lost their native languages, have experienced increased problems maintaining whole families. The more problematic the modern conditions are, the greater the nostalgia for the seemingly simpler, purer and better ways of the past.

Berger has noted that spiritual homelessness has engendered "nostalgias for a condition of 'being at home' in society, with oneself and ultimately, in the universe." A character in Willa Cather's short story, *The Best Years*, states: "I tell you, people are happiest where they've had their children and struggled along and been real folks, and not tourists." The way to combat spiritual homelessness is to be a real person in a meaningful context, and not to see oneself merely as a tourist in life.

Erich Fromm has observed that the modern dilemma has not only generated nostalgia for the past, but has also inspired a certain redemptive yearning for a golden age in the future. He speaks of the counter-modern nostalgias that stem from a rejection of modernity and that seek resolution in the future. Whether one looks to the past or to the future for a golden age, however, one is attempting to find a world restored to order, meaning and group solidarity.

While we certainly need to have a feeling of being at home in the world, we can also grow spiritually by facing feelings of deracination and spiritual homelessness. Escapism to an idealized past or future is a natural, but inadequate, response to the crisis of modernity.

The Spanish thinker, Ortega y Gasset, has written: "And this is the simple truth – that to live is to feel oneself lost – he who accepts it has already begun to find himself, to be on firm ground. Instinctively, as do the shipwrecked, he will look round for something to which to cling, and that tragic, ruthless glance, absolutely sincere, because it is a question of his salvation, will cause him to bring order into the chaos of his life. These are the only genuine ideas; the ideas of the shipwrecked. All the rest is rhetoric, posturing, farce. He who does not really feel himself lost, is without remission; that is to say, he never finds himself, never comes up against his own reality."

The very fact that modernity has uprooted us physically and spiritually means that moderns are in some sense "shipwrecked." We need to draw on our own strengths, take responsibility, make decisions. As Peter Berger has suggested: "Modern consciousness entails a movement from fate to choice." We feel the right and responsibility to take life into our own hands. The modern consciousness does not accept the notion that we are fated to be what we are. In Berger's words: "The taken-for-granted manner in which pre-modern institutions ordered human life is eroded. What previously was self-evident fact now becomes an occasion to choose.... The more choices, the more reflection."

More reflection, though, does not necessarily lead to more happiness. Freedom of choice can be daunting. Many people are afraid to have to make decisions. They prefer to have a charismatic authority make decisions for them. They find it easier to follow the rules of the rat race: conform to the crowd, don't stand alone.

To quote Erich Fromm yet again: "Most people fail in the art of living not because they are inherently bad or so without will that they cannot live a better life; they fail because they do not wake up and see when they stand at a fork in the road and have to decide." To have choices is a great feature of modernity, but one needs to know how to make good choices and then actually have the courage to choose.

This brings us to an interesting feature of human nature. On the one hand, we want the safety and security of a home world; we want to merge our individuality into our home world. On the other hand, we want to be heroic and free, breaking new ground, discovering new worlds.

The Bible teaches that God created Adam from the dust of the earth. Ancient rabbinic tradition offers two interpretations of this mode of creation. One opinion is that God gathered dust from one place, the site of the future Temple in Jerusalem, and from this dust He fashioned Adam. The other interpretation is that God gathered dust from the four corners of the earth to create Adam.

These two interpretations suggest two simultaneous but conflicting truths about the nature of human beings. On the one hand, we are rooted in one place, in one tradition. To be strong and stable, we need to recognize the singularity of our homes. On the other hand, we are created from the dust of the entire world. We reach beyond our own roots; we have imagination, a spirit of creativity, a universalistic outlook. If the creation story teaches us our need to be rooted in one home civilization, it also teaches us our need to grow and to develop our connections with the world at large.

Some people, having an aversion to change, tend to the extreme of conservatism, fearing to move away from their home worlds. Others go to the other extreme; they are enamored of everything new and different. They leave their past behind them with relative ease, even enthusiasm. Winning at life requires us to strike a proper balance so that we avoid these extremes. Let us look more closely at these tendencies.

Some years ago, I read a short item in the newspaper that made a lasting impression on me. The article told of a flood in a country in South America. Flood waters were heading in the direction of low-lying areas, and rescue teams were sent to evacuate those living in the water's path. One team arrived by helicopter at an endangered little farm and told the peasant that they had come to evacuate him. They informed him that his farm was soon to be engulfed by a flood; if he did not leave now, he would be drowned by the oncoming waters.

The peasant agreed to cooperate, but asked the crew to wait for a moment. He then went behind his house and came back with his cow. He told the rescuers that he and his cow were ready to go. Astonished, they told him that he could not bring his cow with him. The helicopter was not equipped to handle the transportation of cows.

The peasant was adamant. He insisted that the cow come with him. The rescuers, conscious of the need to leave quickly before the flood arrived, gave the man an ultimatum: We are not going to take the cow on the helicopter – you must get in yourself. If you do not enter the helicopter immediately, we will leave without you and you will die.

The peasant pondered for a moment and then responded: If my cow cannot come, then I won't come either. The rescuers pleaded with him to change his mind, but to no avail. Unable to wait any longer, the helicopter lifted off, leaving the peasant and his cow behind. Presumably, the man and his cow perished in the devastating flood that soon overwhelmed the area.

My first reaction to this story was to scorn the peasant's sheer, stubborn stupidity. Certainly it would have been emotionally difficult for him to leave his beloved cow to die. But didn't he value his own life above that of his cow? His martyrdom for the sake of his cow seemed ludicrous.

Upon further reflection, though, I saw that the story indicated something deep about human nature. We have a tendency, taken to an extreme by the peasant, to want our lives to be in a familiar context, where we feel at home. For the peasant, his own life was inextricably linked to his farm and his cow. To him, the cow was not simply a dumb anonymous animal. Rather, she was part of the fabric of life as he knew it. The cow provided milk; the cow was a friend, almost like a family member. When informed that his farm was about to be inundated by flood waters, the peasant may have suffered an existential crisis. His whole life was woven into his farm – if the farm were to be wiped out, what would become of him? What would be the meaning of his life? His attempt to bring his cow with him was his way of trying to salvage at least one important element of the framework of his life. Perhaps, together with his cow, he could re-establish his farm after the flood subsided; or maybe he could find a new little piece of land and start another farm. As long as he had his cow, he had a living symbol of continuity with his past. Without that context, he feared that his life would be too painful to bear.

We can now understand, even sympathize, with the peasant's dilemma. Yet, in the final analysis, his decision reflects a mental rigidity that prevented him from adapting to a new and challenging situation. He did not want, or was psychologically unable, to confront new circumstances that would require radical changes in his familiar pattern of life.

The tendency to cling to the old and to fear adapting to the new is evident not only in the case of this peasant, but seems to be a general phenomenon among humans in all strata of society. Adolphe Messimy, the French Minister of War in 1912, attempted to reform the French army uniform in advance of World War I. It had been a cherished French tradition for soldiers to wear blue coats and red trousers. Messimy realized that this colorful uniform was fine in the days when wars were fought by armies facing each other at close range. But with the advent of modern weaponry, armies could shoot at each other from much greater distances. In previous times, it did not matter what the soldiers wore since there was no advantage to being camouflaged. But now, Messimy argued, soldiers needed to wear clothes that would blend in better with the surrounding environment. To wear red pants would make French soldiers bright targets for enemy gunmen.

The suggestion was greeted with howls of protest. People felt that the reform was a blow to the prestige and courage of the French army. A French newspaper protested that to banish "all that is colorful, all that gives the soldier his vivid aspect, is to go contrary both to French taste and military function." A former war minister vehemently opposed Messimy's planned change in military costume, insisting that "the red pants is France!"

The opposition to the change was so great that Messimy reluctantly put aside his proposal. As a result, it is likely that a large number of French soldiers were killed or wounded because they wore red pants while fighting the German army in World War I. Reasonable people could have foreseen this eventuality along with Messimy. But the attachment to the traditional army garb had become a fixture in the mentality of the French public and they were unable to adapt to new circumstances. They viewed reform as an affront to their honor as a nation, to their long-held military traditions.

At the same time, the Russian Minister of War, General Vladimir Sukhomlinov, was a staunch opponent of the idea of "modern war." He believed that "as war was, so it has remained." He prided himself on the fact that he had not read a military manual for the past twenty-five years. He believed that the war then brewing with Germany would be won with the saber, lance and bayonet charge. His inability to imagine that Germany was planning to fight the war with modern firepower cost the Russian army many lives.

These examples reflect the widespread human characteristic of clinging to the old ways and avoiding confrontation with the new. Psychologically, it is easier and more comfortable to stick with traditional patterns, rather than to move in different, untried directions. This tendency, taken to its extreme, has been called by Dr. Norman Lamm "neophobia," fear of the new.

D. H. Lawrence, in his essay *The Spirit of Place*, observed that, "it is hard to hear a new voice, as hard as it is to listen to an unknown language. We just don't listen." The new presents a challenge to the status quo; it causes anxiety within us. In 1531, a wise man admonished the leader of Granada, telling him not to attempt to introduce new things, "for novelties bring in their train anxieties for those who sponsor them and beget troubles among the people." In 1611, the Spanish lexicographer, Covarrubias, defined "novedad" (novelty) as something new and unaccustomed, adding that "characteristically it is dangerous because it sullies traditional usage."

It has proven difficult for humans to change old patterns of thinking and acting, even when these patterns can be seen to be wrong. This characteristic seems to go back even to pre-human history. Anthropologists have theorized that Cro-Magnon beings believed that a certain red powder had the power to bring the dead back to life. They sprinkled the bodies of dead loved ones with the powder, apparently in the hope that they would live again. This procedure, according to these anthropologists, seems to have persisted for at least twenty thousand years, even though they must have realized the futility of this practice at an early point. These prehistoric people, evidently, had the very common human tendency of following traditional authority without challenging its veracity; they were reluctant to evaluate accepted practices with the idea of introducing change.

When human beings are governed entirely by the ideas and habits of the past, they surrender their ability to act freely, to make choices. To learn from the past is desirable; to be enslaved to the past is destructive to our free will. Dr. Silvano Arieti noted that an unthinking commitment to the imperatives of authorities and traditions "cripples the will of man by making him subservient, submissive, conformist, unwilling to change or even try unfamiliar paths."

We have been focusing on the human tendency to keep things as they are and to be suspicious of change. Of course, we also have the opposite tendency – the desire to shake off the yoke of the past and to be innovative. This tendency is given impetus in modern times when there has been a general breakdown in traditional authority and hierarchies. It has been suggested, for example, that philosophy and science were stultified for centuries due to the overwhelming authority granted to Aristotle. Medicine relied on Galen. In many fields, early authorities were considered to have been so great that no later individuals felt the need or the right to challenge them. One of the breakthroughs of modernity was to cast off the early authorities from their pedestals, to challenge old assumptions, to develop new scientific theories and methods.

Modernity has witnessed phenomenal change in the realms of science and technology. The break with past modes is also evident in a plethora of non-traditional art forms, whether in painting, sculpture, architecture, music, dance or drama. Modern literature has explored new styles and modes of expression. Political life has been characterized by numerous new isms and national movements. Even the anarchists of the late nineteenth and early twentieth centuries may be viewed as extreme advocates of radical change. One might say that a basic feature of modernity has been the increased role of rebelliousness, a desire to break away from past patterns.

Erich Fromm has pointed out that the psychic task that a person must undertake "is not to feel secure, but to be able to tolerate insecurity, without panic and undue fear." He added that, "free man is by necessity insecure; thinking man by necessity uncertain." We must confront the conflict between the internal forces of traditionalism and rebelliousness, between idealizing the past or the future. The issue is not whether by clinging to the past or embracing the future we will be able to overcome the existential problem of insecurity and uncertainty. The fact is, thinking people will necessarily have feelings both of connectedness and deracination. The task is to balance these tendencies.

In his novel *The Lost World*, Michael Crichton has captured this dilemma: "Complex systems tend to locate themselves at a place we call 'the edge of chaos.' We imagine the edge of chaos as a place where there is enough innovation to keep a living system vibrant, and enough stability to keep it from collapsing into anarchy…. Too much change is as destructive as too little. Only at the edge of chaos can complex systems flourish." As individuals and as members of modern civilization, we are clearly "complex systems." The edge of chaos is the tightrope that we must walk. Maintaining balance is our imperative.

This chapter has focused on the challenges presented by modernity, as well as the human tendencies to hold on to the past and/or to embrace change, and the need to balance these tendencies so that we do not pursue either extreme. It has been a further exploration in self-understanding by nearing a deeper comprehension of the influences on our core beings. It is also a challenge us to take responsibility for our lives and recognize that we have the ability – and the obligation – to direct our own courses in life. Once we come to grips with the issues raised in this chapter, we will be better able to confront the ongoing pressures pushing us to be part of the rat race.

Chapter Eight

Confronting Suffering and Death

DURING MY MOTHER'S LAST ILLNESS, I used to bring a tape recorder when I visited her in the nursing home. I asked her to reminisce about her past, to tell stories of her childhood and about raising her own children. I also asked her to muse about what she had learned from life. She knew that she was dying, and came to accept – even welcome – the inevitability of her impending death.

At one of those taping sessions, she stated that when one faces the prospect of imminent death, one feels a total sense of honesty and clarity. A dying person no longer has to maintain pretenses or try to win anyone's approval. From the perspective of one who is dying, there is a lot of good in life – but also a lot of nonsense and unnecessary suffering. My mother said: "Facing death gives a better perspective on what is important and what is not important in life."

Fortunately, my mother was a wise and thoughtful person. Throughout her life, she had a very good idea of what was important and what was not. Yet her impending death made her see more clearly how much of life is wasted in needless pain and aggravation. Human society is marred by petty jealousies, vanity, hatred and false pride. During the course of our lifetimes, we may see some things as being very important, worth fighting and even dying for; yet, from the ultimate perspective of one who is dying, those things may now appear to have been exceedingly trivial. They were distractions from life. Those who experience life as a rat race feel a great urgency to win, to get ahead, to win the approval of others; they sacrifice their life energies to attain certain goals. But when these people review their lives with the wisdom gained on the deathbed, will they judge their endeavors to have been truly worthwhile and satisfying?

Let us consider several examples drawn from the rat race of life. To the people involved, their concerns and actions seem of utmost importance. But from the perspective of the deathbed, they strike one as being ludicrous.

When I was a student in college, I returned to my dorm room one morning during finals week after having taken a final examination. To my surprise, I found another student sprawled out on my bed. He was a friend of my roommate, and my roommate was busy fanning him and giving him water to drink. What had happened? This student had been taking a final exam and it struck him that he might not get an A grade on it. He was so traumatized by the possibility of not getting an A in the course that he actually passed out. He was taken out of the room on a stretcher. My roommate had him brought to our room so that the student could regain his composure.

To that student, getting all A grades was of paramount importance. He had to be the best and the brightest. He was in an enormous, self-imposed competition with his classmates. This competition drove him to distraction. When a moment came when he thought he might not "win," he passed out! He simply could not face losing.

This student, who was in fact bright and studious, went on to become a middle level academic, a good professor, though not particularly distinguished as a scholar and author. His career does not appear to be very different from thousands of other academics, even those who had not gotten all A grades when they attended college.

When one is in the rat race, one loses perspective. One makes skewed judgments as to the importance of various endeavors. Only when one steps out of the rat race – hopefully long before one is on the deathbed – does one realize that his judgment had been wrong.

Some people feel the absolute need to live up to external standards of fashion. They will only buy designer clothes. They will spend enormous time, energy and money so that they will find just the right clothes. If they don't obtain these clothes, they feel like failures; they feel ugly; they feel that people are looking down on them. But who made these rules? Why do such people devote so much emotional, physical and financial expenditure to their artificial commitment to fashion? Do they think that no one has anything better to do than judge the clothes they wear? And even if there are catty people who do judge people by their clothes, why should a self-respecting person care about such people's opinions?

When people are in the rat race, they obsess about designer clothes. On their deathbeds, will they think that devotion to designer clothes is essential to living a good life?

The rat race is filled with people who are jealous of others and who feel compelled to criticize, embarrass or gossip about them. They are so insecure of their own virtues, they only feel worthy if they can show others to be unworthy. Their lives are governed by jealousy, envy, greed and revenge. Such people seethe with bitterness. Did they have to choose this pattern of life? On their deathbeds, will they be proud that they wasted so much of their lives driven by these corrupting drives, having caused themselves and others considerable grief?

We all know people who are inveterate name droppers. They think that they impress others by mentioning the important people they know or the famous individuals they have met. They try to validate their own importance by claiming an association with people who are thought to be important. We also know people who are publicity hounds. They crave public recognition and are willing to pay agents high fees to keep their names and pictures plastered in the media. They somehow think that their importance as human beings is measured by how much media attention they receive, rather than by their own internal strength, poise and sense of security.

There is an old joke about a group of women who were bragging to each other about where they went on vacation. Each tried to outdo the others by describing dream trips to faraway lands. Finally, one of the women stated what she thought was the ultimate vacation success story. "Last year," she proudly announced, "we went around the world. This year, we're going somewhere else!" This is the one-ups-man-ship characteristic of the rat race depicted in a humorous spoof.

I once counseled a woman who was a textbook example of the destructive qualities of the rat race. She was so anxious to please her peer group that she could scarcely make a decision without first consulting others. She was afraid to make a choice because she was petrified of falling out of step with her peers. Rather than risk any criticism whatever, she simply did not make autonomous decisions. She would not even laugh at jokes until she first saw that others were laughing. Only then she would join in. What a curse it is to live with this disability! And, in spite of various influences that led her to adopt this pattern, she ultimately was responsible for internalizing it. Why would she cling to a self-destructive quality, one that poisons her life and her relationships with others?

The historian Barbara Tuchman, in her powerful book *The March of Folly*, has contended that governments have been guilty of folly when they followed policies that were contrary to their own interests – even when they had good alternatives available. On the other hand, the summit of good government is achieved "if the mind is open enough to perceive that a given policy is harming rather than serving self-interest, and self-confident enough to acknowledge it, and wise enough to reverse it." What Dr. Tuchman describes as being true for governments seems to be equally true for individuals. The rat race harms self-interest by locking us into a framework that saps our energy, ruins our perspective on matters of ultimate importance in our lives, and stifles our ability to act freely. To break out of the rat race, we must be open-minded enough to recognize the problem, confident enough to confront it, and wise enough to change direction.

The Greek historian Polybius pointed out that, "there are two ways open to all men of changing their ways for the better. One is through their own disasters and one through those of others." It seems that crises force us to confront reality, to see what is genuine and what is counterfeit. In a sense, suffering reduces us to our basic selves – when we face our own mortality, we gain wisdom in the process.

In his work *De Profundis*, Oscar Wilde described his suffering during two years of imprisonment for "gross immorality." Aside from the physical hardships of prison life, he was tormented by feelings of shame, guilt and anger. He contemplated committing suicide as a way of escaping the horrors of his life. However, he came to realize that suffering had meaning and value, that "there is no truth comparable to sorrow. There are times when sorrow seems to me to be the only truth.... Out of sorrow have the worlds been built, and at the birth of a child or star there is pain."

Wilde believed that his experience of suffering taught him humility and provided him a basis by which to redirect his life in a constructive way. By being cast into a prison, he had been deprived of freedom and honor. He could not sustain personal meaning in life by the external props of wealth, social status or fame. At last, he had to consider who he was, what his life should mean. The answers had to be reached from the inner resources of his own being. Here was a human being removed from the rat race, forced to take personal responsibility for the direction of his life.

From suffering and contemplation of death, one may learn to view life with greater intensity. Viktor Frankl, commenting on the frightful conditions of prisoners in Nazi concentration camps – which he himself experienced – observed that "it was possible for spiritual life to deepen." Sensitive people "were able to retreat from their terrible surroundings to a life of inner riches and spiritual freedom."

Dostoevsky once said: "There is only one thing that I dread: not to be worthy of my sufferings." Frankl thought of these words often as he witnessed so many fellow prisoners of the concentration camps suffer and die with a heroic sense of martyrdom. Their suffering and death "bore witness to the fact that the last inner freedom cannot be lost. It can be said that they were worthy of their sufferings; the way they bore their suffering was a genuine inner achievement. It is this spiritual freedom, which cannot be taken away, that makes life meaningful and purposeful."

Frankl stated that the way a person deals with suffering is a measure of the meaning and dignity of one's life. A suffering person can be brave, generous and heroic. On the other hand, a suffering person fighting for self-preservation may become oblivious of human dignity.

While no reasonable person wants to suffer, suffering is an inevitable part of life. The way in which we cope with it is a reflection of our philosophy of life and our moral courage. To maintain "optimism in the face of tragedy" is a means of transforming suffering into a human achievement.

Researchers at the Yale University School of Medicine studied a number of American prisoners who had been captured by the enemy in the Vietnam War. Although these individuals described their captivity as having been filled with torture, disease, malnutrition and solitary confinement, they nevertheless claimed to have benefited from the captivity experience. They came to see their suffering as an element in their growth as human beings.

Rev. Martin Luther King Jr., in reaction to his growing hardships as leader of the civil rights movement, realized that he had two choices. He could become embittered or he could transform his suffering into a positive, creative force. He chose the latter course. He said: "I have attempted to see my personal ordeals as an opportunity to transform myself and heal the people involved in the tragic situation which now obtains. I have lived these last few years with the conviction that unearned suffering is redemptive."

Dr. James Hall, one of the leading psychiatrists in Dallas in the late twentieth century, suffered a debilitating stroke at the age of fifty-seven. He was left in a condition of almost total helplessness, not even able to move his head. His doctors indicated that Dr. Hall would probably spend the rest of his life staring at ceilings. Yet Dr. Hall's mind was intact. He needed to find ways to communicate in spite of his body's inabilities. He learned to type on a computer keyboard, using one finger tied in a splint. In facing his terrible dilemma, Dr. Hall typed the following message: "Life is, if anything, more interesting than before I was disabled. I don't worry now about such things as reputation and earning a living. With essentially nothing to lose, I am more open about what I think."

Rabbi Joseph B. Soloveitchik, arguably the greatest Orthodox Jewish thinker of the twentieth century, contended that there was little point in trying to understand the metaphysical reasons for suffering. For centuries, theologians and philosophers have tried to explain evil and suffering, but all their efforts have yielded unsatisfying results. Rabbi Soloveitchik believed that we should not be as concerned regarding why we suffer so much as how we are to respond to suffering. If we can improve ourselves, deepen our level of wisdom, and reach a greater degree of inner strength, then we have been victorious in our confrontation.

Suffering, then, has redemptive qualities. It tests one's inner strength and spiritual foundations, and deepens one's perception of the meaning of life and death. It can be a turning point, helping one to take stock of life and resolve to live more meaningfully in the future. A serious crisis can be experienced as an advance trip to the deathbed, with all the soul searching and perspective on life that it generates.

Contemplation of our mortality is a sobering exercise. By putting our lives into perspective, it helps us attain humility, compassion and forbearance. The Talmud quotes the opinion of Rabbi Akabya ben Mahalalel: "Ponder on three things and you will not come into the power of sin: know whence you come, where you are going, and before Whom you are destined to give an accounting. Whence do you come? From a fetid drop. Where are you going? To the place of dust and worms. Before Whom are you destined to give an accounting? Before the supreme King of kings, the Holy One Blessed be He." We have humble origins, we have a humble conclusion, and we are held accountable for the way we conducted our lives in the years that were given to us. If we can keep these points firmly in mind, we can avoid falling into the power of sin and stay out of the rat race.

The Bhagavad-Gita, the classic text of Hinduism, includes the following dialogue: "Of all the world's wonders, which is the most wonderful? That no man, though he sees others dying all around him, believes that he himself will die." This dialogue reflects a poignant facet of human psychology. People know theoretically that they will die, yet live their lives with a general feeling of immortality. This illusion preserves a degree of inner peace and optimism. If we constantly dwelled on our mortality, we would be depressed, even neurotic.

Robert Kastenbaum, in *Death, Society and Human Experience*, describes how individuals, especially when young, dissociate themselves from the notion of their own future deaths: "Somebody else who happens to have my name may grow old someday, and may even die. But that's not really me. I am here right now, and I'm as full of life as can be. It's the only way I know to be. I have always been young, never old, always alive, never dead. Sure, I have a good imagination: but to see myself, really see myself as old or dead – that's asking too much." Kastenbaum notes that this attitude is common not only in young people, but also in those who are middle-aged.

Even elderly individuals, who realize intellectually that their deaths cannot be too far off, have the tendency to separate themselves from the notion of their own mortality. They focus, understandably, on their lives today, rather than dwelling on the inevitable death that awaits them.

When my mother was dying, she was perplexed by her perception that she was the same person inside as she had always been; and yet, her body was deteriorating and dying. She emphatically stated that in her inner mind she did not feel old or sick. This is a common phenomenon – that our minds and our bodies are two different elements in our beings.

As my mother's condition worsened, she reached the point that Dr. Elisabeth Kubler-Ross has called "death acceptance." Once a person has fully understood the imminence of death and has stopped struggling against it, then acceptance has been achieved. One faces the conclusion of life with calm and wisdom. Acceptance, as the final stage in the dying process, is often a time of great inner serenity and understanding.

In the normal course of life, we tend to block out the ultimate confrontation with death. We are not pushed to the brink of "acceptance," so we can maintain an illusion of immortality. But it is precisely the clear recognition of our mortality that can teach us the true wisdom of life. Through illnesses and other sufferings, we gain an inkling of this wisdom. We are also drawn to reflections on mortality when we suffer the loss of a loved one.

The author Ben Hecht wrote: "I can recall the hour in which I lost my immortality, in which I tried on my shroud for the first time and saw how it became me.... The knowledge of my dying came to me when my mother died." Like so many others, he was able to internalize the lessons of death vicariously by mourning the death of a loved one. The mourning process challenges us to confront our own mortality, to evaluate what is truly important in our lives, to redirect our life energies to those relationships and activities that are most meaningful. It is the genuine awareness of our mortality that allows us to live life with intensity, sensitivity and calm wisdom.

The Talmud records an ancient Jewish tradition of going to the cemetery in times of extreme crisis. One explanation of this custom is that the cemetery, a vivid reminder of human mortality, naturally makes us more meditative and humble. Recognizing our frailty, we can turn to God with greater emotion, asking for His mercy and loving-kindness.

A second explanation of this custom is that we stand at the graves of our ancestors, praying that God will have mercy on us due to their merit. The lives of our ancestors continue to have meaning and inspiration for us.

Both of these explanations are true. Contemplating the graves of ancestors reminds us to keep our own lives in proper focus, to recognize our own frailty and mortality. It also allows us to remember the lives of loved ones of previous generations and sense their influence on our lives.

When standing at the graves of parents, grandparents, uncles and aunts, and the many other relatives and friends who have passed on, we reminisce about them. We recall happy and sad times, achievements and failures, ideals and values. We very much remember how they confronted suffering, pain and their own deaths. Some were heroic, some less so. Some showed great strength of character, some did not. We remember their numerous sacrifices and travails, their struggles and defeats, and we admire them all the more for having overcome so many difficulties.

Heroism and courage are directly related to the way people handle their adversities and handicaps. The people we tend to admire most are exactly those who have demonstrated strength of character in confronting their sufferings.

Winning at life requires gaining the wisdom and perspective derived from facing our own mortality. This can be achieved by thought and study, by personal experience with suffering, illness and crisis, by mourning the death of a loved one. We need to learn to view our lives now as though we were looking back at ourselves from our deathbeds. By measuring our deeds and words by that ultimate standard, we will be better able to distinguish between what is genuinely important and what is not.

Ecclesiastes wrote long ago: "A generation comes, a generation goes, and the earth abides forever." Each human being is part of this eternal rhythm. From the standpoint of eternity, the life of any one person is like a passing speck of dust. Even the most famous, wise and powerful human beings live a fleeting life; their achievements are of little consequence in the face of infinity.

To recognize our existential smallness is a vital step towards genuine humility. Awareness of our mortality is a precondition to an honest awareness of the significance of our lives.

Chapter Nine

The Pursuit of Happiness

AN ARTICLE IN *The New York Times* (May 19, 2001) was entitled, "If Richer Isn't Happier, What Is?" It pointed out that although Americans are generally much better off economically than they were in the past, their levels of reported happiness have not increased. The average American family received a substantial raise in income between 1970 and 1999, while the percentage of people who described themselves as "very happy" actually declined from thirty-six percent to twenty-nine percent during that period of time.

Various theories have been offered to explain the low level of "very happy" Americans. One argument is that life has become increasingly fast-paced, creating more pressure on people. Another suggestion is that people really are happier, but just do not know it! Their expectations of life have grown faster than their incomes. One survey found that eighty-five percent of Americans wish they could spend more time with their families. Apparently, they feel that their jobs and other commitments are too demanding of their time. Overall happiness in America is also affected by the high divorce rate, and all the related problems that affect those getting divorced, as well as their children.

Americans would seem to be the likeliest candidates in the world to declare themselves "very happy." We live in an affluent, technologically advanced society. Our political system guarantees our rights and freedoms. Indeed, we have so many advantages that millions of people from other countries strive to move to America in order to share in its abundances. And many nations try to emulate American ways, so that their peoples may also enjoy freedom and prosperity.

So why do only twenty-nine percent of Americans rate themselves as "very happy"?

I suggest that the core reason is that our society functions like a rat race, promotes our participation in the rat race, and even idealizes the values of the rat race. In such a framework, it is difficult – if not impossible – for people to be really happy. They enjoy their little victories and celebrate their supposed gains. But in the depths of their hearts, they know that there is a vast difference between a temporary feeling of joy and a longstanding feeling of inner happiness. They also know that happiness is not a goal to be pursued, but is the result of a life well lived.

The eminent scientist, Dr. Lewis Thomas, observed: "One human trait, urging us on by our nature, is the drive to be useful, perhaps the most fundamental of all our biological necessities." Various studies have demonstrated that people want to feel useful, to have a sense of accomplishment, to lead a constructive life.

These goals are achieved by those who have a deep sense of commitment to what they are doing and who believe they are making a valuable contribution to the community.

Along with the drive to be useful – and probably even more significant – is the drive to love and be loved. The many studies on happiness report that married people are generally happier than unmarried people. This does not mean that all married people are happy, nor that all unmarried people are miserable. But it points to the value of a loving relationship based on mutual commitment. Such relationships – rooted in the framework of I-Thou – are deeply satisfying to us. The relative permanence and stability of marriage provide a stronger basis for happiness and fulfillment than temporary romantic encounters that lack long-term commitment.

Another key to attaining happiness is gaining a strong sense of self-worth, a sense that one's life means something and can make a difference to the world. A person needs to feel that when he looks back on life from the perspective of the deathbed, he will feel proud and content at a life well lived. We need to feel satisfaction that we have done our best. Inner strength and moral courage are basic ingredients of happiness.

The rat race undermines the pursuit of genuine happiness. It substitutes quick fixes, superficial thrills and false victories. It fosters standards of success that lead participants to surrender autonomy, denigrate others, and betray themselves. The rat race is an apt symbol for human folly.

To get out and stay out of the rat race requires tremendous commitment, great inner strength, and a transcendent vision of the meaning of life. It entails a life characterized by usefulness, love, self-respect and moral courage. It is easier to speak of these things than to achieve them. They require constant awareness and effort on our part.

We are challenged by the macro-problems of our world: wars, terrorism, racial and religious hatred, poverty and hunger, global warming, destruction of ecosystems – the list goes on and on. As individuals, we often feel powerless to do something that will help change the course of events. Yet we can each do something constructive to improve the world, however small may be our contribution. Despair and apathy must be overcome.

More directly than the macro-problems, we face the everyday challenges of living happily and constructively, of maintaining good and healthy families, good friendships, an ethical business climate, and a compassionate society. William Faulkner, in his acceptance speech upon winning the Nobel Prize for Literature in 1949, stated that writers have the responsibility of reminding each reader "of the courage and honor and hope and pride and compassion and pity and sacrifice which have been the glory of his past." It seems to me that these tasks fall not just on writers, but on all responsible people.

The context of life changes. New inventions, new ways of thinking, new fashions arise. We are bombarded daily with news and information from all over the world. The noisy world of humanity presses down on us.

We are living in what Margaret Mead has called a prefigurative age. We understand what Peter Berger meant when he described the modern phenomenon of "spiritual homelessness." All of us know deep within ourselves that we live in a period of lightning-quick and massive transitions.

Therefore, it is all the more important for us to know who we really are and what we stand for, to see through our own masks and fears and anxieties. We need to get to the "nothingness" within ourselves and begin the process of building ourselves into good, creative and helpful people. By learning from our past, we strengthen ourselves as links in the great chain of being.

As we gain inner wisdom and confidence, we can more intelligently assume responsibility for our lives and for the lives of the coming generations. We can sift out what is valuable from the past and integrate it into our own worldviews. We have the power to overcome negative tendencies that may have been part of our home cultures. As we strengthen ourselves as thinking, feeling human beings, we learn how to better deal with moral conflict, suffering and the ongoing challenges of life. To win at life means getting beyond the rat race.

Can most people accomplish this? Yes, if they apply themselves assiduously to the task. Will most people accomplish this? Probably not. We live in an I-It world where money, ruthless ambition, superficiality and glitz are glorified. The tendencies toward conformity and adoration of charismatic idols are very powerful. Most people do not want to lose the rat race or abandon its rules – even though it destroys their happiness, undermines their morality, and deprives them of the dignity of living free and responsible lives.

Yet here we are, human beings striving to live meaningful lives. Abraham Lincoln well expressed the human enterprise: "I am not bound to win, but I am bound to be true. I am not bound to succeed, but I am bound to live up to the light I have."

I would modify Lincoln's observation: "If I have been true, I have won at life. If I have lived up to the light I have, I have succeeded."

Appendix: Questions for Further Reflection

The text of this book has touched upon a number of topics. The following questions, based on the discussions in each of the chapters, provide a framework for further reflection on these issues.

Chapter One
Losing the Rat Race: Winning at Life

- What are the basic characteristics of the rat race?
- To what extent are these characteristics evident in your life and the lives of your family, friends and associates?
- What are the basic characteristics of winning at life, that can be achieved only by "losing" the rat race? How can you reorient your thinking to focus on ultimate values rather than the immediate pressures of the rat race?
- Have you written an ethical will in which you articulate your vision of the purpose of life? Do your loved ones know what you stand for, what you believe they should learn from you?

Chapter Two

The Rules of the Rat Race

- To what extent should moral and ethical considerations be factored into business dealings? Are you prepared to forego profits in order to maintain your honesty and integrity?

- With what moral conflicts have you been confronted in your business dealings and how have you handled them?

- How charitable are you? Do you contribute at least ten percent of your net income to charitable causes?

- Do you think that you, or those you know, eat of "the bread of shame"? Are you more interested in giving or getting?

- To what extent is competitiveness a positive element in your life, and to what extent is it a negative element? Do you see yourself as being in competition with others, or primarily in competition with yourself; i.e., trying to achieve your own potential?

- Have you been in situations where you conformed to a majority opinion or behavior, even though you felt the opinion or behavior to be wrong? Have you resisted conforming in such situations?

- Do you judge success in yourself and others by material standards; i.e., wealth, physical appearance, popularity? Do you let others set the definitions of "success" and follow along with them? Do you have your own definitions of success that you try to maintain and to convey to others?

- What have been your experiences as part of a crowd?

Chapter Three
The Rat Race for Popularity and Social Acceptance

- Have you avoided or ostracized someone because of the desire to please your peer group?
- What aspects of the intergenerational conflicts within cofigurative cultures are applicable to your family and society?
- Have you ever felt that you have betrayed yourself by conforming to the patterns of your peers?
- How does participation in the rat race rob one of freedom and personal autonomy?

Chapter Four
More About the Rat Race: People as Things

- To what extent are your relationships with others characteristic of I-Thou and I-It frameworks?
- Do you dress in such a way as to encourage I-Thou or I-It relationships?

- If many of your peers dress in sexually provocative, sloppy or defiant styles, do you follow along? Do you have the strength to avoid letting yourself be treated as an object?

- Have you been the victim of irrational discrimination? How have you responded?

- Have you discriminated against others based on their race, religion, ethnicity, nationality, etc.? Why do you have negative feelings against members of such groups? How can you overcome such feelings and try to see them in the framework of I-Thou?

- What are examples of the dehumanization process that are part of your life?

Chapter Five

Starting to Win: Self-Discovery

- Do you devote time on a regular basis to developing your philosophy of life? Do you read books of ethics, moral guidance, philosophy, self-improvement?

- Are you a nonconformist, in the sense used by Emerson? How can you develop or strengthen this quality?

- Did your parents give you feelings of self-esteem and value? What were their greatest strengths and weaknesses relating to your upbringing?

- What are examples of endocratic surplus in your own life? Have you been able to overcome false and destructive notions inculcated into you by parents, teachers and other authority figures?
- Can you distinguish between authoritative and authoritarian figures? Do you yourself fit into either category?

Chapter Six
Memories: Providing Context for Our Lives

- What have been your reactions on seeing old photographs and movies of yourself and your family? Have you visited your childhood home and neighborhood? How have memories of your childhood continued to influence you?
- What lessons may be derived from pondering the experiences of past generations?
- When is nostalgia a healthy, positive quality, and when can it be destructive to one's wellbeing?
- How can you overcome negative feelings you may have about your past?
- Have you demonstrated your own ability to redirect your life and to make changes when you felt you were moving in the wrong direction?

Chapter Seven

Making Decisions and Taking Responsibility

- How does living in a prefigurative culture affect the way you live your life? Do you feel that your "home world" is entirely intact?
- Do you tend toward neophobia or neophilia? How do you strike a balance between these two extremes?
- How have you adapted to new situations – change in job, home, marital status, etc.?
- Do you have trouble making decisions and taking responsibility?
- To what extent is winning at life dependent on directing one's own course in life?

Chapter Eight

Confronting Suffering and Death

- What wisdom can you learn from those who are dying? How can the perspective of the deathbed help you in your own philosophy of life?
- Can you give several examples of how the rat race skews one's perspective on life?
- Have you learned from your own suffering and crises? Have you learned from the suffering and crises of loved ones?

- How does contemplation of mortality help one win at life? How does it put the rat race into proper perspective?
- What are vital characteristics of winning at life?

Chapter Nine
The Pursuit of Happiness

- How do you define happiness? Are you very happy?
- What would make you happier, more content and more fulfilled? What would endow your life with greater meaning?
- Are you useful to others? Do you love and are you loved? How can you improve your relationships with others?
- How do you want the next generations to remember you?
- Do you have the internal strength of character to get out of the rat race and move onto the winning path of life?
- Are you living up to your potential?
- Do you know where you are going?

Bibliographical References

Chapter One

1. Plato. *Dialogues.* Trans. B. Jowett, Roslyn, New York: Walter J. Black Inc., 1942.
2. Bettelheim, Bruno. "Education and the Reality Principle." *Surviving and Other Essays.* New York: Vintage Books, 1980, p. 127.
3. Frankl, Viktor. *The Unconscious God.* New York: Washington Square Press, 1985, p. 91.
4. Berg, Philip S. *Kabbalah for the Layman.* Jerusalem: Research Center of Kabbalah, 1981, pp. 90–91.

Chapter Two

1. McCullough, David. *Truman.* New York: Simon and Schuster, 1992, p. 272f.
2. Asch, Solomon. "Opinions and Social Pressure." *Scientific American* 193 (1955): 31–35.
3. Watts, Alan. *Psychotherapy East and West.* New York: Viking Press, 1974, p. 9.
4. Canetti, Elias. *Crowds and Power.* New York: The Seabury Press, 1978, p. 29.

Chapter Three

1. Coles, Robert. *The Moral Life of Children*. Boston and New York: The Atlantic Monthly Press, 1986.

2. Solzhenitsyn, Alexandr. *The Gulag Archipelago*. New York: Harper and Row, 1973, p. 168.

3. Mead, Margaret. *Culture and Commitment: A Study of the Generation Gap*. Garden City: Natural History Press and Doubleday, 1970.

4. Tan, Amy. *The Joy Luck Club*. New York: Ivy Books, 1989, p. 31.

5. Gandhi, M. *Autobiography*. Trans. M. Desai. New York: Dover Books, 1983, p. 30.

6. Nabokov, Peter, ed. *Native American Testimony*. New York: Penguin Books, 1992, p. 57.

Chapter Four

1. Buber, Martin. *I and Thou*. New York: Charles Scribner Sons, 1958.

2. Fromm, Erich. *Man for Himself*. Greenwich: Fawcett Publications, 1947, p. 249. See also p. 78.

3. Lamm, Norman. "Tzeniut: A Universal Concept." *Haham Gaon Memorial Volume*. Ed. M.D. Angel. New York: Sephardic House and Sepher Hermon Press, 1997, p. 155.

4. Carroll, James. *Constantine's Sword*. New York and Boston: Houghton Mifflin Co., 2001.

5. Levi, Primo. *Survival in Auschwitz*. New York: Simon and Schuster, 1996, p. 96.

6. Frankl, Viktor. *Man's Search for Meaning.* New York: Washington Square Press, 1984, pp. 42–43.

7. Bettelheim, Bruno. *The Informed Heart.* New York: The Free Press, 1960, pp. 127f.

8. King, Martin Luther Jr. *A Testament of Hope.* Ed. J. M. Washington. San Francisco: Harper, 1982, p. 293.

9. Fanon, Frantz. *The Wretched of the Earth.* New York: Grove Press, 1963, p. 41.

10. Fromm, Erich. *The Heart of Man.* New York: Harper and Row, 1964, p. 23.

Chapter Five

1. Kaplan, Aryeh. *Jewish Meditation.* New York: Schocken Books, 1985, pp. 87f.

2. Watts, Alan. *The Supreme Identity.* New York: Knopf, 1972, p. 128.

3. Peck, M. Scott. *The Road Less Traveled.* New York: Simon and Schuster, 1978, p. 24.

4. Fromm, Erich. *The Sane Society.* Greenwich: Fawcett Publications, 1970, pp. 62f.

5. Arieti, Silvano. *The Will to be Human.* New York: Quadrangle Books, 1972.

6. The quotation by Learned Hand is cited by A.M. Sperber, *Murrow: His Life and Times.* New York: Bantam Books, 1986, p. 391.

Chapter Six

1. Calvino, Italo. *Six Memos for the Next Millennium.* New York: Vintage Books, 1988, p. 92.
2. Penfield, Wilder. "Memory Mechanisms." *American Medical Association Archives of Neurology and Psychiatry.* vol. 67 (1952): 178–198.
3. Ferenczi, S. *Sex in Psycho-analysis.* New York: Dover Publications, 1956, p. 6.
4. Lincoln's poem can be found in *The Living Lincoln.* Ed. Paul Angle and E.S. Miers. New York: Barnes and Noble Books, 1992, pp. 87–88.
5. Baxter, Maurice. *One and Inseparable: Daniel Webster and the Union.* Cambridge, Mass.: Harvard University Press, 1983, p. 29.
6. Soloveitchik, J.B. "Kodesh and Chol." *A Reader for Students of Yeshiva University.* 1983, p. 29.
7. Frankl, Viktor. *Man's Search for Meaning.* p. 143.
8. Gruen, Arno. *The Betrayal of the Self.* New York: Grove Press, 1988. p. 60.

Chapter Seven

1. Mead, Margaret. *Culture and Commitment.* See her discussion of prefigurative societies.
2. Berger, Peter and Kellner, H. *The Homeless Mind.* New York: Random House, 1973.
3. Ortega y Gasset, J. *The Revolt of the Masses.* New York: Norton, 1957, p. 157.

4. Berger, Peter. *The Heretical Imperative*. Garden City: Anchor Press, Doubleday, 1979.

5. Fromm, Erich. *The Heart of Man*. p. 138.

6. Tuchman, Barbara. *The Guns of August*. New York: Macmillan, 1962. pp. 37–38 and p. 61.

7. D.H. Lawrence's essay "The Spirit of Place" appeared in the *Norton Reader*, New York: Norton and Co., 1969, pp. 1032f.

8. Fromm, Erich. *The Sane Society*. pp. 174–75.

Chapter Eight

1. Tuchman, Barbara. *The March of Folly*. New York: Ballantine Books, 1984, p. 32.

2. See Frankl's chapter on "The Case for a Tragic Optimism" in *Man's Search for Meaning*.

3. King, Martin Luther Jr. *A Testament of Hope*. pp. 41f. See also p. 212.

4. The experience of Dr. Hall is described in an article by Dee Wedemeyer entitled, "Dr. James Hall, His Life and Mind." *The New York Times Magazine*, August 18, 1996.

5. Kastenbaum, Robert. *Death, Society and Human Experience*. St. Louis: Mosby Press, 1977, p. 41.

6. Kubler-Ross, Elisabeth. *On Death and Dying*. New York: Macmillan, 1975.

7. Hecht, Ben. *A Child of the Century*. New York: Simon and Schuster, 1954, p. 14.

8. Angel, Marc D. *The Orphaned Adult*. New York: Human Sciences Press, 1987.

Chapter Nine

Thomas, Lewis. *The Fragile Species*. New York: Macmillan, 1992, p. 6

About the Author

Marc D. Angel is rabbi of Congregation Shearith Israel, the historic Spanish and Portuguese Synagogue of New York City, which was founded in 1654. He began serving the congregation in 1969. Author and editor of 18 books and numerous articles, his most recent book is entitled, *Remnant of Israel: A Portrait of America's First Jewish Congregation, Shearith Israel* (Riverside Book Company, 2004).

He has been active in a wide range of communal organizations, including the American Sephardi Federation, the Jewish National Fund, HealthCare Chaplaincy, and the UJA-Federation of New York, and is past president of the Rabbinical Council of America. He has lectured widely throughout the United States and Canada, as well as in Israel. He earned his B.A., M.S. and Ph.D. from Yeshiva University, and received his rabbinical ordination from its Theological Seminary. He also has an M.A. degree in English literature from the City College of New York. Yeshiva University conferred an honorary degree upon him in 1992 and he has won numerous awards including the National Rabbinic Leadership Award of the Orthodox Union, the Rabbinical Award of the United Jewish Communities, the Finkle Award of the New York Board of Rabbis, and the Bernard Revel Award for Religion and Religious Education.

He is married to Gilda Angel. They have three children and four grandchildren. Their son, Hayyim, serves as Associate Rabbi of Shearith Israel Congregation.